CW00551100

REVIVAL READY

Rethinking Kingdom,
Discipleship and Church

Steve & Esther Uppal

ALL NATIONS
PUBLISHING

REVIVAL READY: RETHINKING KINGDOM, DISCIPLESHIP AND CHURCH

ISBN 978-1-7390986-0-5

Chapter 1 cover quote taken from *Revival Scenes: Revival Commentary* sermon by Henry Blackaby. Used by permission of Blackaby Ministries International. https://blackaby.org

Chapter 7 cover quote taken from an undated sermon by Billy Graham. Used by permission of Billy Graham Evangelistic Association. https://billygraham.org.uk

Chapter 13 cover quote taken from *Tozer for the Christian Leader: A 365 Devotional* by A W Tozer. Copyright © 2001 by Moody Publishers. Used by permission of Moody Publishers. www.moodypublishers.com

Chapter 15 cover quote taken from an undated sermon by Kathryn Kuhlman.

Chapter 20 cover quote taken from *Daily Inspiration for the Purpose Driven Life: Scriptures and Reflections from the 40 Days of Purpose* by Rick Warren. Copyright © 2010 by Rick Warren. Used by permission of HarperCollins Christian Publishing. www.harpercollinschristian.com

Chapter 22 cover quote taken from *Apostles & Prophets: Reclaiming the Biblical Gifts* by T L Lowery. Copyright © 2004 by T L Ministries.

Chapter 23 cover quote taken from *Crazy Love* by Francis Chan. Copyright © 2013 by Francis Chan. Used by permission of David C Cook. May not be further reproduced. All rights reserved.

Chapter 26 cover quote taken from *Glittering Vices* by Rebecca Konyndyk DeYoung. Copyright © 2009 by Rebecca Konyndyk DeYoung. Used by permission of Brazos Press, a division of Baker Publishing Group.

Chapter 32 cover quote taken from *Don't Waste Your Life* by John Piper. Copyright © 2003, 2018 by John Piper. Used by permission of Crossway, a publishing ministry of Good News Publishers, Wheaton, IL 60187. www.crossway.org

All images accompanying quotes were obtained from photographers on Unsplash.com.

Cover design by Naomi Moyo.

Printed and bound in the United Kingdom by Bell & Bain Ltd.

CONTENTS

CONTENTS

CONTENTS

ACKNOWLEDGEMENTS

We want to acknowledge and thank a number of people who have played a part in getting this book into its finished form. We really could not have done it without them.

Joanne Soh-Kumar for organising and coordinating changing timelines (our fault for missing deadlines) and working with various editors and printers. Your kindness, patience and attention to detail is much appreciated.

Chris Horton for your help in conversations before we started, and in proofreading the final text, thank you.

Naomi Moyo for the cover design and the graphics throughout the book. Thank you for your thoughtful and creative work.

Our daughter Sophia, who is responsible for the creative art throughout the book, thank you so much, you have a wonderful gift.

Our daughter Bethany Milne, thank you for jumping in to help when we were feeling overwhelmed by the project and our schedule. Thank you for typing up the book from sermon clips, notes, voice messages and conversations. We really could not have done it without you. Appreciate you believing in the message of this book and giving sacrificially of your time to get it over the line, while you were heavily pregnant! Mum and Dad love you both.

PREFACE

We have been married since 1997 and have four grown children, our eldest daughter is married, and we have one granddaughter. We have led the All Nations Church Family together since 2001. What began as a local church in Wolverhampton is now becoming a growing family of movements and churches across the UK and into other parts of the world.

In November 2019, the Lord spoke to us clearly that there was coming a *significant season of unlearning*. This was not a comfortable word to hear. At the time, we had multiple services each Sunday, a newly built large auditorium in the city centre, a 24/7 prayer hub, a base in India and several campuses around our region. Everything we were doing seemed to have a measure of success. A few months later, the Lord spoke again and said, '*I am about to change you and you will never be the same again.*' Little did we know what 2020 would hold and how quickly the world and the Church were about to be altered. Everything that we thought we knew and understood was about to be severely challenged.

As we positioned ourselves to listen to the Lord and go deeper in the place of prayer, the two years that followed became the most significant of our entire lives. The Lord spoke more clearly and more frequently than at any other time. It has been an exhilarating and yet deeply challenging journey of rediscovering His heart for revival, the lost, discipleship and church. Paradigms of Church and ministry that had been built over decades have been altered or dismantled all together. Our personal lives have been and are still going through a radical transformation too. Like finding keys to the secret garden, we have stumbled across a life that we did not know even existed. Everything has changed — our marriage, our family and our ministry.

We have written this book with great expectation and in the fear of the Lord. By offering a window into our journey of unlearning old ways and revelations for the new, we pray that you would rediscover ancient pathways and become revival ready. For those exploring the new, this book is a first step in that journey. Before models and patterns change, the Church is required to go through a reforming of its spiritual DNA. This first step of reformation is essential before new programmes, structures and rhythms are embraced. The change in *becoming* will actually lead to *how* and what the Church will do.

We are in the beginnings of a great reformation both in the world and in the Church; may this book help prepare the Lord's people to embrace the coming season well. We would humbly suggest working through the book with others and to do so slowly and prayerfully. Before you read on, we encourage you to pray this simple but dangerous prayer:

> *Lord, help me to see what You see, feel what You feel and to have the*
> *courage to obey.*
> *Amen*

INTRODUCTION

After some deliberation, we decided to divide this book into six key parts reflecting prophetic themes that we felt the Holy Spirit impress upon our hearts. The book could have been structured in a number of different ways, but we felt that these six 'P's provide a helpful framework. Each of the six parts has several bite-sized chapters within it, and each chapter focuses on a different revelation that we have had along the way. These revelations have come from God's Word, times in prayer, dreams, visions and prophecies.

At the end of each chapter there will be a 'What Now?' section and a prayer. Prayer has been a vital thread running through our season of change. The primary method of prayer for us has been to pray Scripture. We are inviting the reader to join us on this prayer journey throughout the book. Our desire is for the Lord to impact your life, not only emotionally and intellectually, but also in a deeply spiritual way that brings lasting transformation.

The first P is 'Promise'. We wanted these initial chapters to set the scene for what we mean by 'revival'. We look at both the biblical and historical precedent for revival, as well as the sure promise, throughout history, that God will visit our lands again.

The second P is 'Process'. These chapters look at the bigger-picture revelations we have had relating to the journey that the Lord is taking us on.

The third P is 'Producing fruit'. These chapters will take you through some of the key actions that we have felt the Holy Spirit leading us to, including the importance of making disciples.

The fourth P is 'Posture'. In these chapters, we explore the ways in which we can best position ourselves while journeying through the process towards the promises of God.

The fifth P is 'People'. These chapters unpack key lessons we have learnt about the fivefold ministry and Kingdom community. People are precious and are God's best strategy.

Finally, the sixth P is 'Pruning'. It is in these chapters that we talk about the challenges we have faced and the pressures we have had to resist.

1. Promise

2. Process

3. Producing fruit

4. Posture

5. People

6. Pruning

At the time when the Lord revealed these six 'P's that make up the new wineskin, He also gave us a further three 'P's that would be necessary for dynamic life to make this a living, breathing wineskin. The new wineskin must be 'Pulsating with Power', committed to only be 'Positioned by the Prophetic' and 'Permeated by His Presence'. We have included a diagram our daughter Sophia drew to help us visualise what we were seeing. We will then conclude the book with a few additional truths for the journey ahead. We have also included recommended books, websites and other resources that have helped us, and we believe can be a rich resource in exploring the themes of this book further.

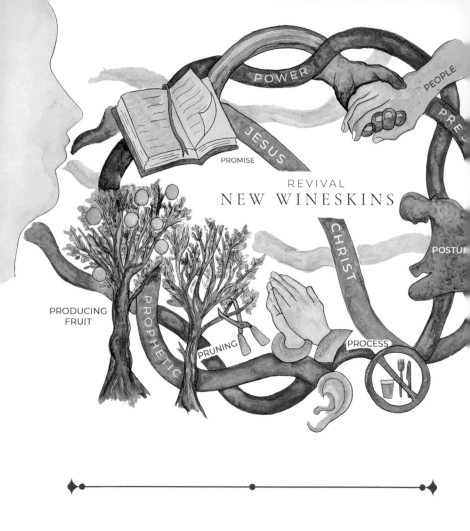

REVIVAL
NEW WINESKINS

PROMISE we hold onto

PEOPLE we are joined with

POSTURE we take

PROCESS we embrace

PRUNING that's essential

PRODUCES fruit

BREATH OF GOD:

Permeated with PRESENCE

Pulsating with POWER

Positioned by the PROPHET

A PROPHETIC HEART-CRY

May God be gracious to us and bless us
And make his face shine on us –
so that your ways may be known on earth,
your salvation among all nations.
May the peoples praise you, God;
may all the peoples praise you.
May the nations be glad and sing for joy,
for you rule the peoples with equity
and guide the nations of the earth.
May the peoples praise you, God;
may all the peoples praise you.
The land yields its harvest;
God, our God, blesses us.
May God bless us still,
So that all the ends of the earth will fear him.

- Psalm 67:1-7

Psalm 67 is not just a poetic scripture, but it is also a prophetic cry as the Psalmist captures the heart of God. We hear within it the deep longing for every nation, tribe and tongue to know and worship God. The Psalmist is asking to be blessed 'so that [God's] ways may be known on earth'. There is no desire for self-promotion, self-preservation or self-advancement, but simply for the glory of God. Our prayer has been that the hearts of believers will beat with the anthem of Psalm 67. Many of today's Christian books, sermons and conversations are centred on personal survival, prosperity and comfort, with hardly a glance at the nations and little awareness of the glory of God. This is changing and an awakening has begun.

Part I: Promise

A promise is a commitment or assurance that someone has made, and that the thing promised will happen. Whether it's a promise of marriage, an inheritance, friendship or something else, promises can bring hope, affect one's emotions and determine one's actions. One's faith in a promise is normally based upon the character and trustworthiness of the person making the promise. The Heavenly Father is trustworthy and has given us many promises. These have huge potential to shape the course of a person's life.

"During true revival, thousands of lost people are suddenly swept into the Kingdom of God. Scenes of the lost coming to the Savior in great, and unprecedented numbers, are common."

- Henry Blackaby

CHAPTER 1 - PAST REVIVAL

When we look at the history of humanity, we see that the human heart has a tendency to drift from its maker. Whether it is Adam and Eve in the garden or the Israelites in the wilderness, when a society forgets God and becomes self-sufficient, it leads to brokenness and pain. But the Lord, in His great compassion, does not forget His people. God can use our brokenness to stir up desperation. As desperate people begin to cry out to God, gripped by a holy dissatisfaction with the status quo, they become gateways for His Kingdom on the Earth. There have been countless moments throughout history where God has stepped into our fragmented world with tremendous power. We call these moments 'revival'.

The pattern of rebellion followed by repentance can be seen time and time again. Perhaps nothing demonstrates it more clearly than the Old Testament storyline of the Jewish people. We see in Psalm 106 and Psalm 107 a snapshot of God's people repeating the cycle of backsliding and then subsequently returning to the Lord.

> But they soon forgot what he had done and did not wait for his plan to unfold. In the desert they gave in to their craving;
> in the wilderness they put God to the test.
> **- Psalm 106:13-14**

Then they cried to the LORD in their trouble, and he saved them from their distress. He sent out his word and healed them; he rescued them from the grave.

- Psalm 107:19-20

We must not doubt God's ability to move based on the sinful condition of our world or how broken our society is. Rather, these things are meant to lead us to come to the Father in prayer and repentance. We can have confidence that as people turn back to the Lord, He always turns to them. In fact, some of the greatest moves of God in the past have broken out in the midst of deep darkness in society. This should give us tremendous hope that in these unprecedented, challenging times there is a heavenly story unfolding.

While looking at definitions of 'revival' can be helpful, we have found that immersing ourselves in historic revival accounts is far more enriching and energising. Whether it is the Hawaiian Revival of 1835, where nearly the whole population turned out to hear the preaching of the gospel; or the Welsh Revival in 1904, where all of Wales was said to be aflame; or the Second Great Awakening, sparked by Mr Charles Finney crying out to God in the middle of the woods; or the Hebrides Revival of 1949, where the churches became packed to capacity and sinners lined the streets to repent. These stories tell of mass conversions, societal transformation and great spiritual renewal. Along with many other revival accounts, they reveal divine moments in history that very few in our generation have ever witnessed. The Holy Spirit will use such stories to stir faith and awaken hearts to the fact that the Lord can do it again. We believe that nothing else can meet the need in our world apart from a genuine Holy Spirit revival that brings transformation to our communities.

What Now?

There is neither space, nor is it the emphasis of this book, to go through detailed historic revival accounts, but we would recommend doing some further reading on this subject. As you read stories from history, allow the Holy Spirit to rekindle hope that what He has done before, He can do again. We have listed some helpful resources in the Further Reading section.

Prayer

> LORD, I have heard of your fame;
> I stand in awe of your deeds, LORD.
> Repeat them in our day,
> in our time make them known;
> in wrath remember mercy.
> **- Habakkuk 3:2**

Thank you, Lord, for the ways You have moved in past revivals. Would You cause faith to rise in my heart that You will do it again? I believe that You are the same yesterday, today and forever. Awaken an appetite in me to see You move in power.

Amen

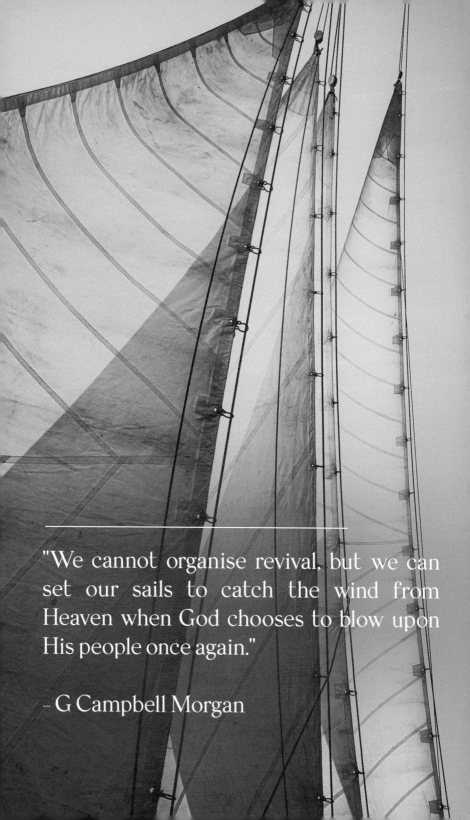

"We cannot organise revival, but we can set our sails to catch the wind from Heaven when God chooses to blow upon His people once again."

- G Campbell Morgan

CHAPTER 2 - PROMISED REVIVAL

We know that, throughout history, God has moved in powerful ways. Yet the greatest stories are not confined to the history books. The greatest stories are yet to be written because the greatest stories are yet to be lived. The Lord always saves the best wine till last (John 2:10). Sadly, many people struggle to see the promises of God as potential realities. We find that they are living merely from experience, habit, the demands placed upon them and submission to the routines of life. This does not have to be the case. Rather we can become a people who see the realities of the Kingdom of God and live expectant with promise. There are many Kingdom promises in Scripture; here are just a few we want to highlight to demonstrate how a person or community could live with these promises:

- In Matthew 16:18, Jesus promised that He would build His Church and that the gates of hell would not prevail against it.

- In Isaiah 43:18-19, we are encouraged to 'forget the former things' as God promises to do a 'new thing'.

- In Isaiah 60:1, we are commanded to 'arise and shine' because of the promise that our light has come.

- In Habakkuk 2:14, there is a prophetic promise that 'the earth will be filled with the knowledge of glory the of the LORD as the waters cover the sea'.

These are kingdom realties to believe and align one's life with. People who have seen the manifestation of the Spirit in revival throughout history have been people who were living in the tension of what was happening around them naturally and yet what had been promised in Scripture. Their prayers and lives became catalysts to bring heaven to earth.

Perhaps one of the most significant biblical promises over this past season for us has been the famous words found in 2 Chronicles. These were the Lord's words spoken to Solomon at the beginning of his kingship and the dedication of the temple. We see a clear pathway set out that can be used to return to God if a people rebel and become sinful.

> If my people, who are called by my name, will humble themselves and pray and seek my face and turn from their wicked ways, then I will hear from heaven, and I will forgive their sin and will heal their land.
> **- 2 Chronicles 7:14**

The pathway is clear and timeless: humble oneself, seek the Lord, turn from sin. It worked in Solomon's day and has been proven in hundreds of communities in the last 2,000 years. We have faith that it will work again today; it will work for whoever will obey the Lord's invitation. He is looking out on all humankind to see if there are any who understand, any who will seek him (Psalm 14:2). He desires to forgive sin and bring healing to our land (Isaiah 44:3). This is a biblical promise for revival that we can actively hold on to with hope.

As well as in Scripture, there have been many significant words spoken over the last 120 years that have prophesied revival and reformation leading to a great harvest of souls. We have picked just two of these to include within this chapter. However, as with the historic revival accounts, we would encourage you to read other prophetic words that have been highlighted in the Further Reading section.

The first one is from **Smith Wigglesworth (1859-1947)**, an evangelist who moved in tremendous power. He gave this prophecy shortly before his death:

> During the next few decades there will be two distinct moves of the Holy Spirit across the church in Great Britain. The first move will affect every church that is open to receive it and will be characterised by the restoration of the baptism and gifts of the Holy Spirit.
>
> The second move of the Holy Spirit will result in people leaving historic churches and planting new churches. In the duration of each of these moves, the people who are involved will say, 'This is the great revival.' But the Lord says, 'No, neither of these are the great revival but both are steps towards it.'
>
> When the new church phase is on the wane, there will be evidence in the churches of something that has not been seen before: a coming together of those with an emphasis on the word and those with an emphasis on the Spirit.
>
> When the Word and the Spirit come together, there will be the biggest move of the Holy Spirit that the nations, and indeed, the world have ever seen. It will mark the beginning of a revival that

will eclipse anything that has been witnessed within these shores, even the Wesleyan and Welsh revivals of former years.

The outpouring of God's Spirit will flow over from the United Kingdom to mainland Europe, and from there, will begin a missionary move to the ends of the earth.

The second one is from **Jean Darnall (1923-2019),** an American minister who had a vision for the UK in 1967.

And what I saw was the British Isles, as in a bird's eye view. A kind of haze was over the whole, like a green fog. And then little pinpricks of light began to appear from the top of Scotland to Land's End. Then the Lord seemed to draw me closer to these lights, and I saw that they were fires that were burning. They were multiplying from the top of Scotland to Land's End. Then I saw lightening [*sic*] come and strike those fires, the brightest spots particularly, and there was a kind of explosion, and rivers of fire flowed down. Again, the sense of direction was from the top of Scotland to Land's End. But some of those rivers of fire didn't stop there. They went right across the Channel and spread out into the Continent…

So many people will be saved, in the villages as well as in the cities, in the schools, in the government, in media, in industry. It will affect the destiny of this nation; it will determine the course of the times.[1]

---

[1] See the full prophetic word in Appendix A.

What Now?

It is essential to allow the promises of God in the Bible and through the prophetic to truly grip our hearts, captivate our imaginations and subsequently inform our world view each day. This does not happen quickly, but it takes time to renew one's mind and take these promises to the Lord in the place of prayer.

1. Take some time to reflect on whether there are any areas in your life that you are doubting God's promises. When it comes to the way you parent, minster or work, are you living from experience and the pressure of others rather than the promises of God?

2. Write down some promises from Scripture and put them in prominent places where you will see them during your daily routine. This might mean changing the lock-screen on your phone or perhaps sticking cards to the fridge. Allow these reminders to help recalibrate your thinking. Praying and declaring the biblical promises is a sure way to anchor them into the core of who you are.

Prayer

For this prayer, we have used the lyrics of a Bethel worship song, 'Prepare the Way':

> We've heard the revival stories
> Of ancient and old-time glory
> Spirit of God, come do it again
> Miracle-working power
> Moving in signs and wonders
> Spirit of God, come do it again
> Prepare the way, He's coming through
> Ready or not, our God's on the move
> We're gonna see, Heaven on Earth
> Come Holy Spirit, awaken Your church.[2]

Amen

---

[2] Extracted from *Prepare The Way*, song lyrics co-written by Dante Bowe, Justin Amundrud, Ethan Hulse, Christopher Cleveland and Bethany Wohrle. Copyright © 2022. Used by permission of Essential Music Publishing LLC, a Unit of Sony Music Entertainment.

"There is no improving the future without disturbing the past."

– Catherine Booth

CHAPTER 3 - A NEW THING

In the last few years, we have been asked on numerous occasions, 'Is God doing something new? And if He is, what is it? What does the new look like?' Our answer is a resounding, 'Yes, God is doing something new and the winds of change are blowing'.

The new has echoes of the old within it but it is not a repeat or replica of what the Lord has done before. Throughout this book we will be sharing some of what we are currently seeing, although we are also aware that the Lord is still in the process of revealing the full picture. We see glimpses of the new and at the same time, we have felt the warning of the Holy Spirit not to finish His sentences. We are not to complete a sentence if He only gives a word, or write a paragraph when He reveals only a sentence. In the past, we have thought that it was good leadership to take what God had said and begin to develop it further. We now recognise that attitude was presumptuous and arrogant. We must not add to His words. It requires a childlike dependence to only move when He leads and speak what He speaks. When we choose to live this way, it develops trust and patience in us.

Some people love change and embrace new ideas, while others are resistant to things they can't fully see. Pioneering new territory is both exciting and challenging. When we were younger, much of what we were doing was new to us. Marriage, parenting and leading a church were areas where we needed fresh wisdom and strong courage as we learned how to navigate unknown territory. After a few years of experience, it was easy to become comfortable and start to settle into established routines.

Over this last season, we have had to make the difficult decision to become pioneers again. The scripture below offers wisdom in how to do just that.

> Forget the former things;
> do not dwell on the past.
> See, I am doing a new thing!
> Now it springs up; do you not perceive it?
> I am making a way in the wilderness
> and streams in the wasteland.
> **- Isaiah 43:18-19**

Forgetting the former things and choosing not to dwell on the past is not easy. Our minds develop ruts, made by regularly travelling the same pathways. We develop certain habits and responses throughout life, work and ministry. These habits can be helpful and make our lives easier and simpler. But as a new season begins, what was once helpful can become a hindrance. Unlearning and forgetting the old ways take an intentional decision on our part, and it can only be done with the help of the Holy Spirit. It is both awkward and humbling to embrace new ways that one is not yet comfortable with.

See It Before You See It

In this Isaiah passage, the Lord challenges His people to see that He is doing a new thing. Reformers and revivalists in Scripture or Church history, are people who have the ability to see what God is doing and are willing to join Him in the adventure. For example, in Joshua 6:1, we read that Jericho was tightly shut up because of the people of Israel. The gates were shut, the walls were fortified and no one was allowed in or out. Despite this reality, the Lord says to Joshua, 'See, I have delivered Jericho into your hands, along with its king and its fighting men' (Joshua 6:2). The Lord was requiring Joshua to see it spiritually before he could see it in the natural. Developing our spiritual eyes by living close to the Lord enables one to see what others may not see. One of our daily prayers is, 'Lord, help us to see what You see and feel the way You feel.'

The promise of Isaiah 43:19 is that the Lord Himself will make a road through the wilderness and cause rivers to flow in the dry wasteland. This is the promise we are holding onto and we are believing that we will see impossible situations turn around. We see the Church becoming healthy, strong and full of God's power. We see a multitude of ordinary Christians leading their neighbours to Christ. We see the Kingdom advance as disciples are made and churches are planted all over the nation. We see the miraculous power of God flowing through ordinary disciples who live extraordinary lives of devotion to King Jesus. We see fires of revival igniting simultaneously across the globe. We see a great harvest of people coming into God's Kingdom.

What Now?

1. Take some time to think about what the Lord may already have been revealing to you. Pray for greater clarity and the courage to embrace new ways.

2. Identify where you may have been resistant to change and write these down. Meet with a trusted friend and pray through your fears or reasons for resisting.

Prayer

The person without the Spirit does not accept the things that come from the Spirit of God but considers them foolishness, and cannot understand them because they are discerned only through the Spirit.

- 1 Corinthians 2:14

Lord, I accept the things of the Spirit. Please help me to see the new thing that You are doing. Open my spiritual eyes and remove every veil that stops me seeing clearly. Give me the courage to step into impossible situations with my confidence rooted deeply in You. In Jesus' Name.
Amen

"New wine must be poured into new wineskins."

– Jesus

CHAPTER 4 -

NEW WINESKINS FOR NEW WINE

We have briefly looked at how God has moved in power throughout history, as well as the promises that He will do so again. This expectation for a transforming revival provides an important context and background for understanding one of the key reasons the Lord is reforming His Church. In preparation for exploring some of the lessons we have been learning for the new thing God is doing, it is important to start with a foundational scripture that became very real to us in April 2020. God spoke to us strongly and repeatedly from Mark 2 that He was about to pour out new wine and that we must have new wineskins to contain it.

> No one pours new wine into old wineskins. Otherwise, the wine will burst the skins, and both the wine and the wineskins will be ruined. No, they pour new wine into new wineskins.
> **- Mark 2:22**

In natural terms, a wineskin is simply an animal skin that is used to hold wine. Over time, these skins can become brittle and inflexible. When new wine, which ferments and produces gases, is poured into old vessels, they crack under the pressure. Not only does the skin become damaged but also the wine is lost. Interestingly, the solution is not necessarily to discard the old wineskins but to restore them. In fact, the word 'new' in the passage from Mark 2 can also be translated 'fresh'. If an old wineskin is cleaned, has the dirt removed and is soaked in oil, it becomes flexible and fit for purpose once again.

In spiritual terms, wineskins represent the people and structures that hold an outpouring of God's Spirit. New wine, therefore, speaks of a fresh move of God. As we look back at Church history, there are many times where movements of the Spirit have led to new structures or ways of doing things. Yet, if we become stuck in our methods and traditions, what was once fresh will begin to resist the new things that God is doing. Such inflexibility will ultimately lead to people getting hurt, churches being damaged and an inability to steward the coming move of God well.

Just as old wineskins can be made useful again, it is good news that the Lord can still work with us if we make ourselves teachable in His hands. People, churches and ministries all have the potential to become malleable. The rest of the book seeks to set out some of the ways we can best submit to His process and, by the help of the Holy Spirit, be made fresh again. We have a firm conviction that God is raising up a new-wineskin generation who will hold their own ideas lightly and have a radical commitment to obedience for the sake of His glory. This is the Lord's doing, and it is marvellous in our sight.

Our Response

For us, becoming malleable has meant spending increased time in prayer. We have asked the Holy Spirit to highlight areas of our life and ministry that will hinder a move of God and the flow of the Spirit. Practically, this has led to rethinking our meeting patterns as a church to help facilitate discipleship (we talk about this more later in the book). In addition to shifting our meeting patterns, we have streamlined our church staff. We wanted to shift the focus from paid staff being 'responsible for ministry' to it becoming the role of every believer in our church family. As Protestants, we have had a theology of the priesthood of all believers, but this has not always been demonstrated in practice.

What Now?

Ultimately, what a wineskin looks like will vary from context to context. The picture of wineskins is not limited to church alone but applies to denominations, movements, leadership teams, marriages and even individuals. The key starting point is a willingness to be flexible in *His* hands and to accept any change the Lord commands.

1. Ask the Holy Spirit to highlight to you areas of your life where you have become rigid and resistant to change.

2. Come up with a list of things that you currently do, as a church, a ministry or an individual, and write down whether they help or hinder the work of the Spirit. Are these activities based on Scripture or do they come from traditions that have formed over time?

Prayer

> Yet you, LORD, are our Father.
> We are the clay, you are the potter;
> we are all the work of your hand.
> **- Isaiah 64:8**

Lord, open my eyes to see the new thing that You are doing, and give me courage to leave behind old structures and mindsets. Prepare my heart that I may be malleable and ready to facilitate the move of God that is coming. I want to be made fresh again.

Amen

"Revelation that is not nurtured
will be lost."

- Steve Uppal

Chapter 5 - Nurturing Revelation

Revelation is simply God speaking to His people and helping us to see things that we did not see previously. While this happens primarily through the Scriptures, we can also hear from God through sermons, an inner witness of the Holy Spirit, prophetic words and dreams, etc. Having been raised in a Pentecostal/Charismatic church culture, we have observed at times a casual attitude in ourselves and others when the Lord speaks. A large part of our recent journey has not only been about applying what we are hearing but also about learning to value and honour revelation. In this chapter, we will look at the importance of nurturing or cultivating revelation.

It is important that we respond well to the revelation that God gives us. If we do not do so, we will lose it; if we nurture the revelation, it can lead to reformation. This can be described as a three-part process. First, relationship with God gives us continual revelation. It is from the place of relationship that He will show us things and reveal what needs to change. Second, if we nurture the revelation, it will begin to change us and we will revolt against the current status quo. Third, as we begin to move in the direction in which the Lord is leading us, we end up with reformed lives, churches and ministry. Relationship leads to revelation. Revelation leads to revolution. Revolution leads to reformation.

As humans, we give value to many things. Some people place a high value on making and having money. Others place a high value on ministry and status. Some people place high value on entertainment and recreation. As followers of Christ, we need to regain a high value for when the Lord speaks. In Psalm 119:72, the Psalmist says that the words from God's mouth are more precious than silver and gold. When God speaks and awakens us to His purpose and His will, it is of upmost value. But in a culture where many use the phrase, 'God said', we can become cynical when the Lord speaks. Guarding against cynicism and cultivating childlikeness is an important discipline for all lovers of God.

One way to show we value what the Lord says is by nurturing the revelation He gives, because revelation that is not nurtured will be lost. We may all relate to times in life when we have felt God speaking clearly to us – perhaps while reading the Bible or when listening to a sermon – but then a short time later we have forgotten what He said and have continued with business as usual. The revelation is forgotten and lost. Perhaps this is a result of being busy and moving on quickly to the next thing on the schedule or because we think that hearing the revelation is sufficient. But hearing revelation is not the same as understanding, digesting and obeying. Revelation is an invitation to respond and to change by aligning one's life to what is being revealed. We must learn to value when God speaks and nurture the revelation given.

How to Nurture Revelation

Proverbs 2:1-5 is a helpful passage and sets out at least six ways that we can respond to what God is saying.

> My son, if you accept my words
> and store up my commands within you,
> turning your ear to wisdom
> and applying your heart to understanding –
> indeed, if you call out for insight
> and cry aloud for understanding,
> and if you look for it as for silver
> and search for it as for hidden treasure,
> then you will understand the fear of the LORD
> and find the knowledge of God.
> **- Proverbs 2:1-5**

First, we must *accept* the revelation. This simply means to acknowledge that God has spoken and to receive His words.

Second, we must *store up* the revelation; we keep it in our hearts and meditate on it. We find journalling helpful.

Third, we must turn our *ear to wisdom*. This may mean asking questions: 'What does the revelation mean?' 'What is required?' 'Does something need to change?'

Fourth, we must *apply our heart to understanding*. Following on from asking for wisdom, applying our heart involves a process of pondering what the Lord has said. Sometimes we do this with others in close community. We have found that the more we live with the revelation, the more detail we begin to see.

Fifth, we *call out for insight and cry aloud for understanding*. This speaks about taking what God has revealed back to Him in the place of prayer, often over a few days, weeks and even months. Praying through revelation is a powerful way for it to become part of our thinking and understanding.

Sixth, we look and *search* for it as for silver and hidden treasure. We often revisit words through conversations with one another and pray over them again. In this way, we train ourselves to actively pursue what God is saying and push deeper because we know that we will find something that is valuable beyond earthly treasures.

Revelation from God shapes and directs people and communities into the most fruitful lives they could possibly have. The Lord speaking is the daily bread we are meant to be sustained by. The promise at the end of the passage is that we will find the fear of the Lord and the knowledge of God. These two rewards are truly priceless!

What Now?

As you read through the rest of this book, take time to nurture the revelation that the Lord gives you. We have included a few practical points for how to do this:

1. Write down the revelation. Perhaps you could set aside a book or journal to keep a record of the things you feel the Lord saying.

2. Pray over the revelation. Take what God has spoken back to Him in the place of prayer.

3. Rehearse the revelation. Read back over what God has said and speak about it with others. The Holy Spirit will rest on such conversations.

4. Seek counsel over the revelation. We hear God best when we hear Him together. Ask others to speak into it: 'Am I right?' 'Is this the Lord?' 'Is there something more?'

5. Obey the revelation. If God is asking you to do something, respond in obedience.

6. Don't rush through the book but find the pace of the Spirit.

Prayer

This prayer is taken from Psalm 119:129-136:

> Your statutes are wonderful;
> therefore I obey them.
> The unfolding of your words gives light;
> it gives understanding to the simple.
> I open my mouth and pant,
> longing for your commands.
> Turn to me and have mercy on me,
> as you always do to those who love your name.
> Direct my footsteps according to your word;
> let no sin rule over me.
> Redeem me from human oppression,
> that I may obey your precepts.
> Make your face shine on your servant
> and teach me your decrees.
> Streams of tears flow from my eyes,
> for your law is not obeyed.

Amen

Part II: Process

There have been multiple phrases and sentences that we have felt the Holy Spirit give to us. These have often come in times of prayer and in conversations with others on the journey. As Jesus used parables, some of these phrases use imagery that allows us to understand deeper truths. There is some overlap in the revelation, because God often says the same thing in numerous ways to enable us to see and grasp the full picture. The next few chapters relate to the bigger picture of what the Lord has been doing with us. We pray that they are helpful in understanding the process that He has been taking us through.

"Believe God's word and power more than you believe your own feelings and experiences. Your Rock is Christ, and it is not the Rock which ebbs and flows, but your sea."

- Samuel Rutherford

CHAPTER 6 - PROMISE VS PROCESS

P romise and process go hand in hand, but it is often easier to get excited about prophetic promise than to appreciate the necessary process. We long for revival, and the salvation of souls. We desire for our neighbourhoods to be transformed by the power of the gospel and to run into the new of what the Lord has for us. But between the promise and the fulfilment of that promise is often a wilderness of the exact opposite. The journey between the two is God-ordained and essential for our maturity. It is in the wilderness that the Lord prepares His people, getting them ready for the promise. The wilderness is an essential place for the formation of God's servants.

Many Christians live with the mindset that because they have received Christ and attend a church, things should just work out for them. They give way to the wrong understanding that God's will and promises are automatic and their lives will now be enhanced with ease and comfort. This kind of idealism leads to disillusionment and discouragement. From the moment of salvation, we are to be a people who commit to learning how the Kingdom of God works and must be willing to embrace biblical process towards maturity. Society around us expects things to happen quickly, from food delivered within minutes, instant mobile banking or the calling of a taxi. This cultural mindset is prevalent in Christ-followers and tempts us to rush the process instead of valuing the journey as an opportunity for growth, change and preparation.

The process to the promise brings about transformation on the inside; this cannot be rushed because it takes time for a person and thereby an organisation to change. We are not simply playing around the edges with new programmes or models of church to brighten things up a little. Rather, the Church is undergoing a significant change to its spiritual DNA so that God's people can become all that He intends them to be. We are in the midst of a major reforming (reformation) of the Church, and the Lord is not in a hurry but will do a thorough work.

In a culture that places high priority on instant results, it has been helpful to remind ourselves that this has not been the way of the Lord's people throughout history. We have found great encouragement from the stories of different Bible characters that the Lord has highlighted to us along our journey.

Noah was given the promise of a flood and commanded to build an ark that would be the form of protection for him and his family. Between the command to build and the first signs of rain was a period of 120 years, and up to this time, it had not rained on the Earth before. There were probably people who mocked his efforts and there were perhaps times when he doubted whether the flood would ever happen. Yet, sure enough, the rains came and Noah and his family were saved.

David was anointed to be king by Samuel while still a young boy in the fields. He then went through more than ten years of hardship before seeing the promise come to pass. He was hunted by King Saul who wanted him dead, and spent his time on the run, living in caves. Yet, true to God's promise, David was anointed king over Israel just as the Lord had promised. The wilderness was God's training ground for David.

Joseph was given dreams of leadership as the favourite son in his father's house. It took 13 years of betrayal, slavery, false accusations and prison before he stepped into the fulfilment of this promise. Again, when the Lord felt Joseph was ready, Joseph became second in command over the most powerful nation on the Earth at the time and saved his family and many others.

Moses was born to be a deliverer of the people and had been miraculously protected as a baby. After escaping Egypt, he spent many years hidden away in the desert as a shepherd, with no sign of his prophesied calling in sight. It wasn't until he was 80 years old that he saw the people of Israel delivered. Yet, true to the promise, he led Israel out of Egypt and out of slavery.

Jesus Himself was born into the world to save it from sin. He came to fulfil prophetic promises that had been spoken hundreds of years before His birth. Those prophecies predicted where and how He would be born and the salvation He would bring. Yet His first 30 years were a hidden life as a carpenter before He began His ministry. Three decades of waiting, faithfully serving the family business and living in obscurity. Sure enough, the promise of the Lord was fulfilled, and Jesus became the Saviour of the world.

The Lord is never in a hurry. Who we are becoming is far more important to Him than what we are doing. It is our character that carries our gifting. When we embrace the journey and allow His process to form character in us, we can have confidence that the Lord is faithful to fulfil His promises. We see from each of the biblical examples that it was faithful obedience in the small things that led to increased opportunities. Noah faithfully built the ark; David faithfully tended his father's sheep; Joseph was faithful in the service of Potiphar and in the prison; Moses faithfully tended Jethro's flock and Jesus lived a life that attracted the pleasure of the Father (Matthew 3:17), while waiting 30 years to begin His ministry.

They all allowed the process to form servant-hearted, humble obedience in them, while keeping a clean and tender heart. Being servant-hearted is an important characteristic for us as we journey through the process. They were also being enlarged on the inside through difficult trials. We will look at the importance of humility, obedience and Christlikeness later on in the book and we encourage you to delve deeper into these themes.

In summary, servants submit to the Father; they are teachable, people of integrity, selfless, trustworthy, accountable, alert and obedient. Jesus said of Himself that He did not come to be served but to serve (Matthew 20:28). If we are to embrace the process, we must embrace the nature of a true servant. The Lord Jesus is cleaning His house, just as he did in Matthew 21:12. There is a purifying work that the Lord is doing within His Church because much of the world and its ways have crept into our lives and ministries. He gives a promise and then takes us through a process towards that promise.

What Now?

1. Write down some of the ways that you have felt tested as you have waited for the promise.

2. Are there things that have happened that seem to be the opposite of what the Lord has spoken? Ask the Holy Spirit for help to grow through these things. You could ask, 'Holy Spirit, what is it You want me to learn or change?'

Prayer

Out of his fullness we have all received grace in place of grace already given.
- John 1:16

Father, thank You that You give me grace. Help me to embrace Your process so that I may be prepared for the prophetic promise. Thank You that what You are doing in me is more important than what You are doing through me. I want to look more like You each and every day. I desire the nature of Christ to be formed in me and to see the trials and the wilderness periods as opportunities to grow.
Amen

"Any other foundation will fail, but Christ is a sure and steady rock to build your life on."

– Billy Graham

CHAPTER 7 - FOUNDATIONS FIRST

T hough we rarely stop to admire the foundations of a building, having the right foundations in place is absolutely essential. There is a temptation to focus our energy and attention on what can be seen, on the structures above the surface, but it is the foundations of a building that determine its height, strength and longevity. The same is true for the spiritual foundations of an individual, a couple, a family or a church. As we have started our journey to the new, we have been challenged to do deep foundational work first.

1 Corinthians 3:11 tells us that the only foundation that can be laid is the foundation of Christ. Unlike foundations under a building, which are built once and then remain static and lifeless, when we talk about spiritual foundations, we are talking about that which is living. Christ is the living cornerstone upon which the Church is built (Ephesians 2:20). The Early Church knew what it was to lay the foundation of Christ. In the first five chapters of Acts, we see the disciples refer to Jesus time and time again. They preached Jesus, prayed to Jesus, healed in His name, and shared His teaching. Similarly, the Apostle Paul, when writing his letters to the churches, had Christ as the central theme. In 1 Corinthians 1, there are more than ten references to Jesus in just the first nine verses. He was to them a living, leading person necessary for each decision and every movement.

Contrary to the example of the early believers, many churches today have been built on things other than Jesus Christ. Perhaps it is the foundation of charismatic leaders, latest models for growth, changing worship styles or preaching methods. For some it is the foundation of social justice work or pastoral care. These things are not wrong and will probably play a part in the life of a Christ community, but in themselves, they cannot replace the foundation of Christ. Jesus must be central in how we make decisions, what we say and the actions we take. The phrase 'foundations first' is really an invitation from the Lord to re-lay the true biblical foundation of Christ. We must do this before we can even begin to look at the other aspects of building church.

There are five aspects to laying the foundation of Christ, and they are all interconnected:

1. The Person of Christ

2. The Work of Christ

3. The Teaching of Christ

4. The Mission of Christ

5. The Spirit of Christ

First, we build on the foundation of His person. Jesus Christ is the foundation of the Church (1 Corinthians 3:11). In Colossians 1:18, Jesus is described as the 'head of the body, the church'. He is a living and speaking God whom we must know and walk intimately with every day. He is calling us from faith in programmes to faith in the person of Jesus Christ.

Second, we build on the foundation of His work. There are many aspects of what Christ has done that will take a lifetime to explore, not as dry theology but as living truth that shapes our lives. He has reconciled us to the Father (Colossians 1:20); He has made us 'the righteousness of God' (2 Corinthians 5:21); He has dealt with sin and death (Romans 5); He makes us one with the Father (John 17:21); He brings us into a new Kingdom, a new culture and a new value system (Colossians 1:13). Jesus is still interceding for us at the right hand of God (Romans 8:34). Part of laying the foundation of Christ is understanding what the cross has accomplished for us and is still actively working.

Third, we build on the foundation of His teaching. Many sermons today are based on human ideas and strategies, often designed to meet short-term material or emotional needs for the listener. There must be a return to the teachings of Christ. Human ideas will fall away but the teachings of Jesus are eternal. Jesus spoke about the Kingdom of God, its values and its ways. Whether in the Beatitudes, the parables or His commands, we must not only hear and be familiar with these truths but make them the firm foundation of everything we build. Jesus said, in Matthew 7:24-27, that those who hear His words *and put them into practice* will be like a wise man who built his house upon the rock. Hearing the teachings of Jesus is not the same as obedience. Obedience is obedience.

Fourth, we build on the foundation of His mission. His mission is to set people free (Luke 4:18). His mission is to destroy the devil's work (1 John 3:8). His mission is to make disciples of all nations (Matthew 28:18-20). His mission must become our mission. Many Christian people are giving their lives mostly for their own personal mission, whether that be to have a rewarding job, earn a good salary or raise a respectable family. These things are often gifts from God that we steward and enjoy, but they don't release us from the call Christ places on every one of His followers. We were created to take up the mission of Christ and we will find the greatest satisfaction and eternal reward when we do. If we seek first His kingdom and His righteousness, everything else will be added to us as well (Matthew 6:33).

Fifth, we build on the foundation of His Spirit. We can only build on His person, His work, His teaching and His mission by the help of the Holy Spirit. The Spirit is our counsellor and is the promised gift of Jesus in John 14. Having a daily relationship with the Holy Spirit is not an option but a necessity, and it is a very real way by which we grow our relationship with Christ. Many people are rediscovering the joy of walking in the power of the Spirit day by day.

These five ways of building are Kingdom ways to lay a secure foundation. Psalm 127 makes it clear that unless the Lord builds the house, those who build it labour in vain. We must not build on anything other than the foundation of Jesus.

Get the Outdoor Work in Order

> Put your outdoor work in order
> and get your fields ready;
> after that, build your house.
> **- Proverbs 24:27**

During the lockdowns in 2020, we, and it seems many others, found time to do work in our garden. A broken gate needed strengthening and a new lock needed adding; the shed needed to be stripped back and repainted; rubbish from recent building work needed clearing away; a bench needed restoring and seed needed to be sown to patch up the grass. These were all foundational things that were necessary preparation to get the garden ready for planting. In the same way, God is wanting us to get our lives in order, to create access and strip away things, to repair foundations and remove rubble from the past. How we clear space and lay foundations will impact what we can grow in our garden for the future. Foundations are vital to be revival ready.

What Now?

1. Make time for growing your relationship with Jesus. He will only be foundational in our lives when we know Him and know His voice.

2. If you already have a daily devotional time, ask the Father for greater intimacy during these times.

3. If you don't regularly have time with the Lord, set aside a daily time to speak with Him and hear from Him through His Word.

4. Remove faulty foundations. Prayerfully consider, with people you love and trust, whether there are things other than Jesus on which you are building your life. Surrender these to the Lord.

5. Obey. As we briefly looked at the parable of the wise and foolish builders, we see that strong foundations come from putting Jesus' words into practice. Take one thing from Jesus' teaching (this could be a Beatitude or a lesson from a parable) and ask the Spirit to help you implement it in a practical way this week.

Prayer

For no one can lay any foundation other than the one already laid, which is Jesus Christ.

- **1 Corinthians 3:11**

Father, I thank You that when the correct foundation is in place, everything else is built steady and strong. I recognise that Jesus Christ is the only foundation I can build my life upon. Would You help me to lay the foundation of Christ – His person, His work, His teaching, His mission, by the power of His Spirit.

Amen

"I consider that the chief dangers which confront the coming century will be religion without the Holy Ghost, Christianity without Christ, forgiveness without repentance, salvation without regeneration, politics without God, and heaven without hell."

- William Booth

CHAPTER 8 - STOP, RESET, RECALIBRATE

Like passengers in a high-speed car driving down the motorway, it felt as if the brakes had suddenly been slammed on and we were jolted forward. The spring of 2020 began with a 'STOP', a hard and sudden halt. Hospitality, entertainment, work, holidays and sporting events all came to a standstill. No one could have predicted that the world would stop as it did or how long it would last.

While we don't believe that God created Covid-19 and recognise that there was much pain, devastation and loss caused by the enemy, yet at the same time, we do believe that God can work through any situation that the enemy is engineering, to His own advantage and ultimately for our good. We believe that Covid-19 provided *a divine 'stop' to interrupt our activities and wake up a sleeping Church*. We had become so busy with our routines and programmes that there was neither time nor space to hear clearly. Suddenly, we were forced to be still and listen to His voice. The Father was speaking.

Following the 'stop' came the 'reset'. 'Reset' simply means to set again or to set differently. When a smartphone stops working and becomes glitchy, you may try a soft reset by turning it off and on, and many times this resolves the issue. If the problem still persists, the manufacturer recommends that your phone needs a hard factory reset. A hard reset deletes all data, including personal preferences, and resets the phone back to the manufacturer's original design.

We began to realise that the Church, like a glitchy phone, was not functioning as the Maker had originally intended. Rather than producing disciples, the Church had become personality-driven, platform-oriented, Sunday-centred and consumer-focused. Perhaps, like personal preferences on a phone, we had even grown to like some of the features that were leading to dysfunction. Rather than live with a Church that is not obeying the Great Commission by making disciples and is mostly void of New Testament power, the Lord is inviting His Church to return to His original design. We find this design in His manual, the Word of God. The rest of this book will look at what this means in practice; in summary, *the Lord is reinstalling a radical obedience to the Great Commission and the making of disciples.*

Following the 'stop' and 'reset', we felt the word 'recalibrate'. To calibrate an instrument or tool means to adjust the readings so that they come into alignment with a standard scale. This allows for accurate measurement. For too long, the Church has been using its own varying standards to measure success. The Lord is recalibrating the Church back to the standard of His Word by the help of the Holy Spirit to measure in the light of eternity.

In Revelation 3:17, we see a stark discrepancy between the way that the Laodicean church viewed itself and the way that the Lord viewed it. The church in Laodicea measured its success by its wealth and affluence, yet the Lord described it as 'wretched, pitiful, poor, blind and naked'. In verse 18, He counsels its people to buy salve for their eyes so that they may see.

How many churches are living with a false sense of security because their view of success is different to the Lord's? We must have His eyes and begin to measure accordingly.

Lockdowns have lifted and our lives have resumed some normality. We may have learned to live with the glitches in our systems, perhaps even preferring them. We may even be content with our limited, self-measured 'successes', but the Lord is still inviting His Church to stop, reset and recalibrate. It is not just an optional exercise but a necessary process if we are to become revival ready and obey the King's teaching in the New Testament.

Another reason for the reset is because we are about to see the greatest harvest of souls come into the Kingdom. In its current form, the Church cannot handle and care for those who are coming. The Lord loves us deeply and will do whatever is necessary to awaken and prepare us ready for the days ahead.

The world is also changing. Hostility and persecution are prevalent and will increase in the days ahead; the stability of the economy is in question and there is a sense of global unrest evidenced by riots, protests and wars. The pandemic was the first of many birth-pains that have begun on the Earth (Matthew 24:8). Unless the Church stops, resets and realigns, it will not survive the increased shaking that is coming.

What Now?

God is so gracious. He 'is not slow in keeping his promise, as some understand slowness. Instead, he is patient with you, not wanting anyone to perish, but everyone to come to repentance' (2 Peter 3:9).

Perhaps, in reading this, you feel that you missed out on the pause that came during the pandemic. Perhaps you had glimpses that He might be up to something but did not respond at the time. It may be that this is the first you have heard about God inviting His Church into a stop, reset and recalibration. Wherever you find yourself, it is not too late. There is an invitation from the Holy Spirit to say yes to all that He is doing. The response starts with each individual; you do not have to wait for others before you respond to the Lord. Each of us will ultimately have to stand before the Lord on our own and give an account for what we have done with what He has spoken.

1. Make time to stop. Set aside some time, even this week, to pause and reflect on what you're doing and the road you are currently heading down. Are you making disciples through your life? It can be helpful to journal your thoughts.

2. Prayerfully read through Acts 2:42-47. Divide a piece of paper into two sections. On one side, write the title, 'Things I am currently doing', and on the other side write, 'Things I am not yet doing'. Write down each of the activities listed in the passage, and there should be at least 13, on the applicable side of the paper. This can be a helpful way of assessing whether our lives need resetting to God's intended design for the Church.

3. Ask the Holy Spirit to recalibrate your thinking. Be open to the fact that the way you have been measuring success may not be the way God sees it. Make it a daily prayer that the Lord would renew your mind to see things as He does.

Prayer

> This is what the LORD says:
> "Stand at the crossroads and look;
> ask for the ancient paths,
> ask where the good way is, and walk in it,
> and you will find rest for your souls.
> But you said, 'We will not walk in it.'
> **- Jeremiah 6:16**

Father, please give me the courage to STOP busy activities long enough to hear Your voice. Give me salve for my eyes, that I may see what You see about myself, my family, my marriage and my church. I want to become revival ready, but I need Your help. Would You lead and direct me and show me the way I should go.

Amen

"We are awakening to that marvellous truth,
that Christ is not in the heavens only,
nor the atmosphere only,
but Christ is in you."

- John G Lake

CHAPTER 9 - INVITATION TO INTIMACY

When we talk about the 'process' that God has been taking us on, there is a temptation to want a formula: 'If we do x and y, God will do z.' In some ways, if this were the case, it would be much easier. However, we have not been given a dry formula. This has been the default for many churches and leadership conferences over the last few decades and it is difficult to break the mindset. Rather, we have been given some key principles and an invitation to intimacy. It is a mind-blowing reality that the Creator of the universe would choose to operate in such a personal, relational way.

Prayer is the mechanism for intimacy. The importance of prayer cannot be overstated, and we must not limit it to our past experience. Prayer is not just a good biblical theme; it is absolutely the most important part of the journey that we have been on and essential for the new thing God is doing. It is only from the place of prayer that we have known wisdom in making decisions, peace when faced with conflict and strength for the journey. We cannot overstate the importance and value of prayer. Prayer, however, is not a means to an end, though much is accomplished by prayer; communing with God is the end itself.

If you had asked us a couple of years ago, we would have probably said that we had the prayer thing sorted. As teenagers, we would hold prayer meetings before school, in lunch breaks and even all-night prayer meetings with friends. Over the years, the subject of prayer has been prominent within our church community. By 2017, we were growing our way to a 24/7 prayer hub and there were many faithful prayer warriors calling on the Lord day and night. We were both praying for a couple of sessions a week in the prayer hub individually. Yet, looking back, we had begun to excuse ourselves from a deeper commitment to the place of intimate communion with God. The demands of a growing family, a large multi-site church and busy international ministry seemed like legitimate reasons.

It was during the first Covid lockdown that we decided to pray together in a more intentional and extended way. There was suddenly no travel, no meetings and nowhere to go. This meant that we could spend unhurried moments in God's presence in a consistent and daily way. We decided to pray from 4am to 6am every weekday. At the start, we thought it would not be sustainable. But we believe the Lord gave us a few months of tremendous grace where His presence came strongly and revelation was rich. He was awakening our appetite and showing us how it could and should be. Now, we realise, we cannot sustain our life, ministry or marriage unless we pray like this.

After more than 25 years of marriage, this commitment to pray together for two hours each day has been the most significant thing that we have ever decided to do. We have experienced a richness and reward from the place of intimacy with Jesus that is unlike anything else. It has unlocked a new and deeper way of life, and we believe every human is created for this kind of intimacy with God.

Yet I hold this against you: you have forsaken the love you had at first. Consider how far you have fallen! Repent and do the things you did at first. If you do not repent, I will come to you and remove your lampstand from its place.

- Revelation 2:4-5

Jesus invites us to live in an intimate place of love with Him. Naturally speaking, conception takes place during the intimacy of a couple. In the spiritual, it is no different. When we have intimate communion with the Lord, things are conceived. Revelations of Himself, His grace and His unconditional love become real to us in these moments. In the presence of God, we begin to see the world differently, we see ourselves differently and we find that our behaviours begin to change. Just like Zacchaeus in Luke 19, when we spend time with Jesus, there is total transformation in our thinking, behaviour and values. Living in God's love causes us to experience a significance based on friendship rather than function. When we spend time in intimate communion with God, we begin to change, to be transformed into the likeness of Christ.

The Bible tells us that Jacob worked seven years for Rachel but it seemed like a few days because of his love for her (Genesis 29:20). Working for the Lord, even in difficult circumstances, takes on a sweetness when we are rooted in the experience of His unconditional love. The place of intimacy is where the Lord has designed for us to abide in. Without love, our work becomes laborious and makes us weary. On the other hand, lovers make the best workers because their labour is prompted by love.

The Bible uses the picture of marriage as a way of describing a believer's relationship with Christ (Ephesians 5:21-33). In a healthy marriage, love grows as it is cultivated. This happens through conversation, repentance (changed thinking), forgiveness and time in each other's presence. Love deepens and the relationship grows stronger over time. The intentional turning of the heart towards one another keeps the fire burning. Of course, this can also work the other way and love can grow cold through offence, independence, isolation, unforgiveness and neglect. Relationships are like gardens that need careful nurture and much time. A person's relationship with God is no different; with the help of the Holy Spirit and careful nurturing it can become a beautiful place of safety, intimacy and flourishing.

~

Below is a story written by Esther that we felt was relevant to include here:

> I remember when our four children were small and Steve was travelling on a ministry trip abroad into a semi-closed nation. I missed him greatly and wanted to hear his voice, to see his face, but we had not been able to connect for a few weeks. I was struggling and it caused me to lose my appetite. I asked God to help me to be mature, and I never forget the response God gave me. He showed me that our marriage was a picture of Christ and the Church, that I was supposed to love Steve this much and that He wanted the Church to have its first love restored, that it should cause the Church to struggle and lose its appetite when it can't hear God's voice or feel Him close.

On most ministry trips, Steve would call home often and speak with the children. Near the end of a trip, he would ask them what they wanted him to bring back for them. I observed as they got older, they would stop asking for things. The answer they gave became, 'We just want you.'

Phone calls have been great over the years, and Facetime even better. But the best is when Steve walks into the house – in that moment nothing else matters, everything can wait and all is well. May we desire God like this. We long to hear His voice and see His face, but His presence is what makes all the difference.

We can get excited by stories of how God has moved throughout history. We can get excited by the promises of revival. We can get excited about the transformation of the Church or seeing the lost come to know Jesus. But we miss the point if we do not first get excited about Christ Himself. It is time for the Church to mature and for us not only to seek what we can get from God but first to desire Him.

The Great Commandment, to 'love the Lord your God with all your heart and with all your soul and with all your mind' (Matthew 22:37), is really a call to great intimacy. Unless we return to the place of intimacy, through prayer, we neglect the most important thing. God is love and He calls His people to love Him first and to love Him most. It is a staggering thought that the uncreated, self-existent God would want to know us intimately.

As you continue through the rest of the book, we pray that it would all be read in the light of this important backdrop: intimacy with God.

What Now?

1. Set aside a regular, daily time to pray. Whatever your current prayer life looks like, set a goal to increase this. You can also join in with our All Nations Movement Global Prayer Hub[3] to receive prayer points and live interaction with others praying on a particular day.

2. Believe God, that He is able to meet you in a way that you have not yet experienced. If you have not known the joy and delight of prayer, ask the Holy Spirit for this. It is a biblical promise that when we ask, we will receive (Matthew 7:7).

3. Do some further reading on the topic of prayer using the resources listed in the Further Reading section. There has not been space in this chapter for in-depth teaching on prayer. We have only scratched the surface. You can also access free eCourses on prayer on our All Nations Storehouse platform.[4] Why not work through these as a family or in a smaller group?

---

[3] See https://allnationsmovement.org/prayer for further information.

[4] See resources on disciple-making under the Further Reading section. https://anstorehouse.org/

Prayer

Jesus replied: "'Love the Lord your God with all your heart and
with all your soul and with all your mind.'

- **Matthew 22:37**

*Father, thank You for the privilege of prayer. Thank You that You are inviting
me into a place of intimacy with You. I count it a privilege that You,
the uncreated, self-existing God, would invite me to know You. Would You
help me not to be more excited with new ideas than I am with You?
I ask for a grace to cultivate a deeper, richer prayer life.*

Amen

"God brings men into deep waters not to drown them but to purify them."

- James H Aughey

CHAPTER 10 - SHAKEN TO PURIFY

At that time his voice shook the earth, but now he has promised, 'Once more I will shake not only the earth but also the heavens.' The words 'once more' indicate the removing of what can be shaken – that is, created things – so that what cannot be shaken may remain.

- Hebrews 12:26-27

Early on during the pandemic, we felt reminded of these verses in Hebrews 12. The New Testament passage is directly quoting from the book of Haggai. In both the Old and New Testament passages, there is a prophesied shaking of the heavens and the Earth. The purpose of the shaking is to remove that which cannot be shaken so that only the eternal, unshakeable remains. We believe that the pandemic was one way that the Lord was shaking the Earth.

There are at least five categories of shaking that we believe Matthew 24:8 refers to as 'birth-pains'. There is economic shaking, political shaking, geophysical shaking (earthquakes, famines, hurricanes), religious shaking and social shaking (protests, wars and rumours of wars). Jesus warns us that, because of such wickedness on the Earth, the love of many Christians will grow cold. But those who stand firm to the end will be saved (Matthew 24:12-13).

While we can often be quick to blame the devil for all such problems, it is clear from both Hebrews 12 and Haggai 1 that sometimes it is the Lord Himself who shakes things up. He will use discomfort, and even pain, to purify His Church.

Just like when Jesus walked into the temple, made a whip, overturned tables, released birds and scattered coins (John 2:13-16), a disruption to what we know is coming because many have allowed idolatry into their lives and churches. Idols can take many forms, and much of the Western mindset and value system has crept into the lives of Christians and influences the way we build His Church. It happened in Jesus' day and it is happening again today.

There are a lot of human-made structures, human-made ideologies and human-inspired value systems within the Church, and we may not even realise it. Whether it's our love of entertainment, our holding of opinions that are contrary to the Scriptures or our inclination for popularity and comfort, much has crept in that needs to be shaken off. There has also been the idolatry of leadership and strategy, taken from the world and brought wholesale into our thinking, training and planning. Many leaders in the Church hold similar if not identical values to those who don't know Christ, idolising fast growth, big platforms, large numbers and looking for the next secret sauce to grow the Church. Yet contrary to these values, Jesus was born in poverty and obscurity and spent most of his life misunderstood and hunted by the establishment.

As we have stated earlier, the Lord is cleaning His house, and this isn't always comfortable. Just like in Mark 11:17, Jesus is once again calling His Church to become a house of prayer for all nations. We do believe multiple thousands will come into the Kingdom and there will be very large churches and movements emerging, but they will look more like the Early Church rather than corporate companies.

The things that will survive the shaking are those things that really matter in the light of eternity. Though we can be quick to place our emphasis on physical things, whether that be buildings, platforms, congregations or events, it is often the unseen that has the greatest eternal value. Our relationship with the Lord really matters. Our relationships with others really matter. Our obedience to the Father really matters. True worship really matters. Our character really matters. The way we love really matters. These are some of the things that will remain and must be top priority for us.

With purity comes the restoration of true authority and power for Christ-followers and for His Church. Please see the prophetic word given in 1987 by Pastor David Minor in Appendix B.

What Now?

As we feel the discomfort of the continued shaking around us, we must ask ourselves whether there are things in our life that need removing. Are there attitudes that we have or habits that we live with that need to be removed? Are we prioritising those things that really matter in the light of eternity?

1. Read through the Beatitudes in Matthew 5:3-12 and the fruit of the Spirit in Galatians 5:22-23. Both these passages are great examples of attitudes and behaviours that will remain and withstand the shaking.

2. Ask the Lord for His help to develop the nature of Christ in your life and for the courage to let go of all that is human-made and needs to fall away.

Prayer

Create in me a pure heart, O God,
and renew a steadfast spirit within me.
- **Psalm 51:10**

Lord, give me the courage to let things fall away that are not from You. Would You help me to embrace the ways of Your Kingdom, Your value system, and to spend my energy on that which will remain in the light of eternity? Amen

"Let us not be surprised when we have to face difficulties. When the wind blows hard on a tree, the roots stretch and grow the stronger. Let it be so with us. Let us not be weaklings, yielding to every wind that blows, but strong in spirit to resist."

- Amy Carmichael

CHAPTER 11 - SHAKEN TO AWAKEN

Wake up! Strengthen what remains and is about to die, for I have found your deeds unfinished in the sight of my God.
- **Revelation 3:2**

As well as the shaking leading to a purifying of the Church, we also felt that the shaking had another purpose. Multiple times we heard the phrase, 'shaken to awaken'.

When our eldest son was little, he would often fall asleep at the dinner table. We didn't want him to sleep at this time because we knew it would mess up his sleeping pattern. After trying several techniques of singing loudly round the table or calling his name, we found that the most effective approach was to gently shake him awake. We would take him from his high chair, open the back door, carry him into the garden and move him around in the fresh air. Though it may have felt uncomfortable for Joel, it was precisely the discomfort and change of scene that kept him awake.

Similarly, when a fire bell sounds in a school, children are trained to respond with urgency, to leave behind all belongings and assemble in the correct place. It is often uncomfortable, cold and inconvenient. A spiritual alarm is sounding in our day, and it requires an urgent response to leave everything behind and embrace the discomfort which in turn will awaken us. Being where God wants us to be is the safest place.

We believe that, through the shaking in the world, God is purposefully awakening His children. He does this because He loves us and wants us to make the most of the times in which we are alive. The Lord is speaking loudly and clearly, but only those who are fully awake will understand what He is saying. 'Whoever has ears, let them hear what the Spirit says to the churches' (Revelation 3:22).

In the letters of 1 and 2 Peter, we see the phrase used many times, 'be alert and of sober mind'. Here is one example:

> Be alert and of sober mind. Your enemy the devil prowls around like a roaring lion looking for someone to devour. Resist him, standing firm in the faith, because you know that the family of believers throughout the world is undergoing the same kind of sufferings.
> **- 1 Peter 5:8-9**

Here are some of the reasons why Peter is repeatedly challenging the believers to be sober, or awake, and alert.

- So you can resist the enemy

- So you can stand firm

- So you may be watchful

- So you can pray (1 Peter 4:7)

The Church must have an alertness and sobriety. It is only when we live in this way that we can be watchful and resist the enemy who is coming against us.

You Snooze, You Lose

Waking up is not enough. There is a real danger that we can fall back to sleep. Another phrase we felt the Lord give in line with this sleeping analogy, was, 'You snooze, you lose.' The snooze button on an alarm allows an individual to have a few extra minutes of sleep even though it is time to wake up. The danger of snoozing is that the comfort of warm, familiar surroundings lulls a person into a false sense of security and before long, they go back to sleep, unaware of the true time. Sometimes that snooze button can be pressed repeatedly until the person sleeping becomes oblivious to it.

Practically, hitting the snooze button means going back to the lifestyle that we may have felt challenged about. There are lots of things in the world that can lull us to sleep. The entertainment of the world can creep into our homes for more hours each day than the life of the Spirit does. This constant feeding on the world is putting the Church into a sleepy state. There is a significant line in the film *Braveheart* where the main character refuses to drink a bottle of strong pain-numbing medicine before he is about to be tortured. He says to the princess who offers him the bottle that he needs all his wits about him. The Church needs all her wits about her and all her senses fully awake. We must stop medicating with the things of this world that keep us in a state of slumber.

Many in the Church have heard the Spirit's wake-up call in their lives but have reached for the spiritual snooze button. Whether it is the pull of pragmatic voices or the comfort of the familiar, choosing to defer action will lull you into a false sense of security and cause spiritual slumber. An individual or a church can be busy, noisy and active but still be lukewarm and fast asleep.

When the alarm sounds, respond immediately and with a whole heart. Waking up and staying awake are both equally important. If you snooze, you could lose.

~

Below is another story about our elder son, written by Esther, that we feel parallels what God is doing in the spiritual.

'Wake up, Joel, it's 7am. It's time to get up and ready for school.' A muffled reply came back. 'Wake up, Joel, it's 7:30am! It's time to shower and dress.' There was a growing urgency in my voice now. Nodding, he opened his eyes in partial acknowledgment of my request. I returned a few moments later with greater desperation and firmness to my voice, 'Wake up, Joel! You must get up or else we will be late!' This became a daily conversation as we journeyed through the teenage years.

It was a busier morning than usual and as we piled into the car at 8:15am to leave for the school run, I had an awful feeling. Where was Joel? Was he still in . . .? Surely he couldn't be? We had all made so much noise. Leaving the other children in the car, I bolted up the stairs to find Joel in a deep, peaceful sleep. What had happened to the little boy who had always been up at the crack of dawn? I shook him awake and with great speed grabbed him a banana and a drink to have on the journey.

This was it for me. I soon decided to include the whole family in my daily endeavour to wake up Joel. The children were excited and enthusiastic to join me in waking up their brother. Judah thought that pulling his big brother by his feet off the top bunk bed was a great idea (although this was not encouraged nor well received). Bethany sang loudly to awaken him, and Sophia teased Joel by telling him it was later than it actually was. Steve probably got the quickest response as he blasted music from a speaker. Waking up Joel had become the responsibility of us all. It was a family effort.

Often, when Joel would finally get up, he would say something like, 'Why didn't you say something earlier to wake me?' It is interesting that we cannot always hear or remember what God is saying to us when we are half asleep.

The Lord awakens us in numerous ways - challenging circumstances, conversations with others, the Bible, sermons we hear and much more. There have been a number of calls to the Church in the West to be fully awake but, just as Joel did not heed the call, so many are not paying the attention that they should be.

In sharing this story, we feel it is significant that our son is called Joel. The prophet Joel prophesied about an outpouring of the Holy Spirit in the last days (cited by Peter in Acts 2:16-21). He is waking us up to prepare us for an outpouring of His Spirit, and we must not drift back to sleep.

The greatest enemy of hunger for God is not poison but apple pie. It is not the banquet of the wicked that dulls our appetite for heaven, but endless nibbling at the table of the world. It is not the X-rated video, but the prime-time dribble of triviality we drink in every night.

- John Piper[5]

What Now?

Choosing not to dull our senses with the things of this world is a great way of staying alert and awake. Some suggestions for how to do this are below. It may be tempting to view the list as legalism or rules. This should be avoided. These disciplines are deeply relational, and only if we do them from a place of relationship will we be able to sustain them.

1. Place yourself among those who are awake. The company you keep determines the spiritual sleepiness or wakefulness that you will live in. If you surround yourself with prayerful, fiery people, this will sharpen you and you will become a prayerful, fiery person. Proverbs 27:17 tells us, 'As iron sharpens iron, so one person sharpens another.' We must make intentional decisions to be around these sorts of people.

2. Quieten the noise of the world. How will you reduce your exposure to entertainment, socialising or recreation to make more space to hear the Lord?

---

[5] John Piper, *A Hunger for God* © 1997, p. 18. Used by permission of Crossway, a publishing ministry of Good News Publishers, Wheaton, IL 60187. www.crossway.org

3. Build in regular rhythms of prayer and fasting. Both these disciplines will keep us in a wakeful place. Whether it's one or a couple of days a week, it is going to become more normal for the Church to embrace a regular fasting lifestyle.

4. Meditate on the Word of God throughout the day. Read a passage and allow it to serve as water that washes, a hammer that awakens or a mirror that helps you to see.

Prayer

> This is why it is said:
> 'Wake up, sleeper, rise from the dead,
> and Christ will shine on you.'
> **- Ephesians 5:14**

Lord, I ask for Your revelation light to wake me up from my sleep so that I may hear Your voice and help to awaken others in Your family, the Church. May I be sober minded and alert so I can resist the enemy, remain watchful and pray fervently.

Amen

Part III: Producing Fruit

In this section, we look at some of the revelation we have had around producing spiritual fruit. Many believers have become used to fruitless lives or seeing very little fruit in their lives. We often make excuses for why this is the case and subsequently set the bar in Western Christianity quite low. The standard of how we should live and the fruit we should produce is determined by King Jesus Himself. In John 15, Jesus clearly states that He wants His disciples to bear much fruit, and fruit that remains. Both quantity and quality matter to Him.

When we talk about fruit, it can be summed up in two broad categories. First, fruitfulness is having the character of Christ. Second, fruitfulness is producing disciples who live in obedience and in turn, make disciples. The new wineskin is people, and the condition or quality of those people is very important to the Lord. He deeply loves His bride, the Church, enough to bring her to a place of fruitful maturity.

"A soul filled with large thoughts of the
Vine will be a strong branch, and will abide
confidently in Him. Be much occupied
with Jesus, and believe much in Him,
as the True Vine."

- Andrew Murray

CHAPTER 12 - ABIDE IN ME

Remain in me, as I also remain in you. No branch can bear fruit by itself; it must remain in the vine. Neither can you bear fruit unless you remain in me.

- John 15:4

This passage from John 15 makes it clear that the only way we can bear fruit is by remaining or abiding in Christ. To remain is to continue to exist in and to stay connected to something or someone. The Church has not always been good at this, nor have we realised our need to remain. Perhaps this is because we have not truly believed it's possible to live in the abiding place with Christ. The Church needs living examples of men and women who walk closely with the Lord, but these role models have been few and far between. Over the last few years, we have begun to see this change and are encouraged to see radical lovers of God emerge. This is necessary to help young and new disciples to be raised in godly communities.

It is easy to look at the busyness or activity of a person or a church as fruitfulness. Being busy with activities, even good activities, is not the same as being fruitful. Many church projects and initiatives have been born from a place of human strategy and discussion and not from the Spirit's leading in the place of abiding. A crowd is not fruit. Big buildings are not fruit. Slick programmes are not fruit. Even having someone raise their hand at an altar call is not necessarily fruit. Unless we learn to remain in the Father and in His Word, we won't be able to discern what He is desiring to produce in us and what is simply human-made.

We could use any of the words 'remain', 'abide' or 'live'. They all speak of what a person is most conscious of, or aware of. We all abide somewhere. We can abide or remain in a state of worry. We can remain in a worldly narrative that is strengthened by the voices of the media, work, entertainment and news. We may be caught up with the status quo of church and ministry. Without an intentional commitment to obey the words of Christ and to remain in Him, it is easy for a person to live for hours, even days, unaware of the Lord's nearness, love and voice. Jesus commands us to remain in Him, in the awareness of His reality, life and love. It is important that we choose to live in Christ and not in any of these other things.

As you reflect back on the last week, where have you mostly lived? Throughout history, men and women of God who have brought about change for His Kingdom have done so as they have lived in Christ. It is from their connection to the Father that their perspectives begin to change and they see the world as He does. They lived on earth while setting their hearts and minds 'on things above' (Colossians 3:1-2).

Remaining or abiding is about living in the active experience of God's love. It's the awareness of His love, and accepting and believing that He loves us and has good in store for His children; therefore, our words matter, our actions matter. Also, it is understanding that He is not distant but close and wanting to help us be fruitful.

Abiding begins by accepting His words; therefore, if His words are to remain in us, we must make sure we are regularly reading the Bible, which is His written Word. There can be no remaining in Christ until there is a commitment to living in His Word. Of course, His Word refers to the Bible as a whole, but there is also a special importance in knowing the words of Christ in the Gospels. From our personal experience, the more we live in the Word, the more our hearts turn towards Him and we are aware of what He is asking us to do. The Bible is one of the most powerful tools to help us stay on track and live in the abiding place.

If you abide in Me, and My words abide in you, you will ask what you desire, and it shall be done for you.
- **John 15:7**

If we are to remain in Christ, we must first believe that it is possible to do so. We have come across many people who doubt that they could live in a constant abiding place with the Lord. We recognise that it is a challenge to live this way; nevertheless, it is possible. Jesus does not ask us to do something that we are unable to do; rather, He comes alongside to enable us. 'What is impossible with man is possible with God' (Luke 18:27).

It is not that we have to stop all our normal activities and isolate from the world in order to be with God; we can remain in Christ while living full lives. One of our heroes over the years has been a monk named Brother Lawrence. He wrote about how, even as a very busy monk working in the kitchens, he learned how to practise the presence of God. Practically, he learned how to turn his attention towards the Lord throughout every moment of a day. We can do the same, turning the activities of our work and relationships into worship. As a person lives in this place, the Lord gives wisdom, strength, direction and joy.

Who may ascend the mountain of the LORD?

Who may stand in his holy place?

- Psalm 24:3

Perhaps you have experienced what it is to be in God's presence for short bursts of time following a powerful meeting, conference or devotional time. These moments of encounter are invitations to a way of life. In Psalm 24:3 the Psalmist asks, 'Who may stand in his holy place?' There is an invitation not only to 'ascend the mountain of the Lord', but also to stay with Him. In Psalm 91, we see again the invitation to rest in the shadow of the Almighty.

Whoever dwells in the shelter of the Most High

will rest in the shadow of the Almighty.

- Psalm 91:1

If we are to see lasting fruit produced in our lives and tap into divine help for everyday living, we must learn the secret of abiding. Perhaps there have been days, weeks or months that have passed since you have felt connected to Him. Do not allow this to discourage you. Rather, see the invitation of the Father, to reset and go again. He is smiling and He is waiting with hands outstretched.

What Now?

1. Where are you living? Take a moment to reflect on whether you invite God to share in what you are doing or thinking.

2. Practise turning your affection towards the Lord throughout a day. Ask the Holy Spirit to remind you of His nearness as you do the school run, peel potatoes, go to work, mow the lawn or whatever else you find yourself doing. Remember, His presence is with you. Whisper a prayer to Him: 'Thank You that You are here. I choose to remain in You today.'

Prayer

So then, just as you received Christ Jesus as Lord, continue to live your lives in him, rooted and built up in him, strengthened in the faith as you were taught, and overflowing with thankfulness.
- **Colossians 2:6-7**

Father, thank You that You created me to be deeply connected to You in the vine. Help me to remember that I can bear no fruit on my own. Thank You that You want to help me and empower me. Would You grant me grace to practise Your presence and learn to abide with You?
Amen

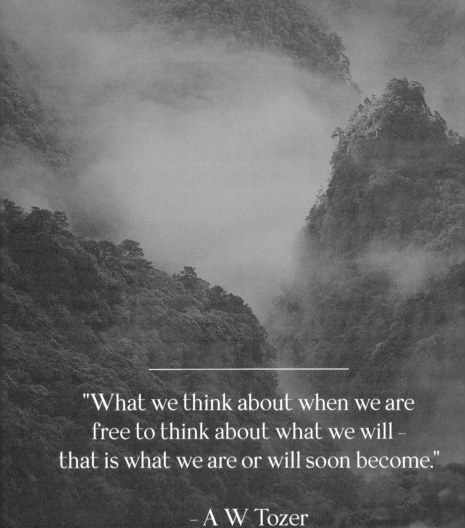

"What we think about when we are
free to think about what we will –
that is what we are or will soon become."

- A W Tozer

CHAPTER 13 -
CULTIVATING CHRISTLIKE CHARACTER

The command to be fruitful can be traced right back to the Garden of Eden (Genesis 1:28). In John 15:8, Jesus said that bearing much fruit is how we show ourselves to be His disciples and how we bring the Father glory. While we have felt the significance of this command for the Church as a whole, namely in her ability to produce disciples, we have also felt the real challenge of this command in relation to our individual lives.

There have been many times over the past two years that we have felt the Holy Spirit put His finger on different attitudes and character traits that we had been living with that needed to change. Whether it is entitlement, jealousy or pride, we have felt a heightened conviction of the Holy Spirit to align our lives to the nature of Christ. We have tried to be diligent in responding and repenting of things as the Lord reveals. This has not been an easy process, but we believe that forming Christlikeness in His people is a big part of what God is doing in preparation for the coming revival. To become like Christ is one of our highest callings in life.

Many people today value works over character. We are often quick to applaud the gifts of the Spirit, whether that be healing, prophecy or words of knowledge, but are less excited by the demonstration of the fruit of the Spirit in a person's life. We may share a link on our social media to a dramatic prophecy but are less likely to celebrate the person who has been faithfully married for 40 years, has raised their children well and is living free from debt. We live in a world that is enamoured by charisma but does not value integrity and character. This can be seen in our politicians, film and music stars, and, sadly, now our church leaders.

Character really matters to the Lord, and it should really matter to us. It doesn't take much digging through recent Church history to find examples of people with exceptional gifts but whose poor character caused major problems in their marriage, finances or abusive treatment of others. This has been damaging to the Church and her reputation. When we live as Christ did, we set an example to the world around us of what it means to follow Him.

The life and attitudes of Jesus can really be summarised in the fruit of the Spirit that we read in Galatians:

> But the fruit of the Spirit is love, joy, peace, forbearance, kindness, goodness, faithfulness, gentleness and self-control. Against such things there is no law.
> - **Galatians 5:22-23**

Throughout the chapter in Galatians, we see the stark contrast between a life governed by the Spirit and a life governed by the flesh. While we are all on a journey, it is clear that there is not a middle ground for us to camp in. Either we are dead to the flesh and alive to Christ or we are alive to the flesh and dead to Christ. Outward expressions – how we spend our money and time, for example, or how we respond to our spouse and others – are often indicators of where a person's heart is. In Matthew 7:16, Jesus said that 'by their fruit [we] will recognise them'.

We will bear the fruit of the Spirit when we live in step with the Spirit (Galatians 5:25). 2 Corinthians 3:16 says, 'whenever anyone turns to the Lord, the veil is taken away'. A couple of verses later it says, 'We all, who with unveiled faces contemplate the Lord's glory, are being transformed into his image with ever-increasing glory.' Here we see a promise: whenever we turn to the Lord, whether through the Word or through prayer, every veil will be removed; we will see more clearly and we will be transformed into His image. We must learn to turn to the Lord; as discussed earlier, this really is the abiding place. The Holy Spirit is the Helper who produces this lifestyle in us as we submit to Him.

We have found that prayerfully reading the Bible, with an awareness that the Author is present, is a great way to turn to the Lord and realign our heart and attitudes. This washing in the Word of God helps us to continually see the lifestyle we should be living. Alternatively, if we spend all our time immersing ourselves in the world's value system, we can begin to justify certain attitudes and behaviours that we see modelled through media outlets. The way of the world is not the way of the Kingdom. We must become more familiar with the narrative of the Lord than we are with the narrative of the world; this forms in us a biblical world view. As we learn the ways of the Kingdom and adjust our lives to the way of the King, we also grow in our authority. Remember, this is a deeply relational, two-way interaction with our Saviour through the work of the Spirit. It's not a 'try harder and change yourself' effort.

Another way we keep in step with the Spirit is by responding to the inner witness or prompting of the Spirit. There have been many times, whether it be in meetings with other leaders or around the table with family, that we have heard the inner voice of the Spirit challenging an attitude or a response that we have just had or given. Whenever the Holy Spirit makes our own wrong attitudes apparent to us, we ought to repent of them and ask for His help to put things right. If the effects of our attitudes have been felt by others, it is also necessary to apologise to them. Learning to say sorry and making frequent adjustments towards godliness is a way of living a fruitful life. Responding well to conviction keeps a person tender before the Lord and allows them to be malleable in His hand. It's these small yet consistent course corrections that help us to become more like Jesus.

The new wineskin is people and transformed people will be the ones to contain the new wine. Becoming like Christ is therefore essential if we are to be good vessels to steward the coming move of God. Circumstances, situations, tough times and our responses to them are all part of the journey towards transformation. Transformation can be for better or for worse. We are either becoming more like Christ each day or less like Christ; it's not likely that a person stays in a static place. We have to be intentional if we want to be transformed into the likeness of Christ. It does not happen accidentally or automatically.

What Now?

1. Pray through the fruit of the Spirit listed in Galatians 5 and ask the Holy Spirit to make them alive and evidenced in your own life.

2. The Beatitudes found in Matthew 5:3-11 are Kingdom characteristics that should be in the lives of Christ followers. Listing and praying through these is also a helpful way to understand what it means to be like Christ.

3. Are there things in your life that you need to turn away from? Why not take time today to do that?

Prayer

And we all, who with unveiled faces contemplate the Lord's glory, are being transformed into his image with ever-increasing glory, which comes from the Lord, who is the Spirit.

- 2 Corinthians 3:18

Father, thank You that You work transformation in me by the power of the Holy Spirit. I want to be a fruit-bearing person and I want the life of Christ to be evident in me. I ask that my friends and family would see Jesus in me and glorify the Father. Help the fruit of the Spirit – love, joy, peace, patience, kindness, goodness, faithfulness, gentleness and self-control – to be strong in my daily life.
Amen

"You are not here in the world for yourself.
You have been sent here for others.
The world is waiting for you!"

– Catherine Booth

CHAPTER 14 - DISCIPLES MAKE DISCIPLES

One of the key challenges we have felt during this season is the importance of making disciples. For many years, we have given altar calls in our meetings and seen people make commitments to follow Christ. This is great and exciting, but has often produced converts rather than disciples. As we look back, we reflect on how we have been able to fill our auditorium with hundreds of people over multiple services each week at our church gatherings. These are good people who profess faith in Christ as their Saviour, but not all have come to Christ as King or Lord. We have preached the gospel of salvation with little focus on the gospel of the Kingdom. The gospel of salvation offers forgiveness of sin and eternal life. The gospel of the Kingdom calls a person to forsake their old ways, come to King Jesus, take up His mission and obey His teaching.

Many in the Western Church try to live morally good lives, give money to the Church and perhaps serve in a ministry area. There is nothing wrong in these things, but being a morally good person who gives financially and serves in some capacity is not necessarily the same as being a disciple of Christ. The Great Commission of Jesus in Matthew 28 is not to make converts, church attenders, morally good people or volunteers. The Great Commission is to *go* and make *disciples*.

It is paramount that we understand what a disciple is, become disciples ourselves and reproduce disciples if we are to obey Jesus. It is only as we do this that we become truly fruitful.

What Is a 'Disciple'?

A 'disciple' literally translates as 'apprentice'. It is somebody who comes alongside to learn from another. Disciples were common in Jewish culture before Jesus' time. There is an old Hebrew saying, 'May the dust of your rabbi rest on you.' The idea was that disciples would live so close to their rabbi, or teacher, that even the dust from their feet would kick up and rest on them. The primary way that disciples learned was not through classrooms or books but by living in close proximity to their teacher.

We see this modelled with Jesus and His disciples. They walked with Him, ate with Him and travelled with Him. By staying near him, they became like Him. In Matthew 4:19, Jesus says, 'Follow me … and I will send you out to fish for people.' It is in following Him that we are made into who we should be.

How Do We Become Disciples?

Today, as always, a disciple of Christ is one who follows Him closely, who knows Him personally and who is committed to becoming like Him. Just as Jesus was committed to revealing the Father and spreading the message about the Kingdom of God, so will His disciples be. Disciples of Christ will connect people to the Father and manifest the Kingdom of God wherever they go.

At the height of His ministry with the crowds following Him, Jesus said in Mark 8:34, 'Whoever wants to be my disciple must deny themselves and take up their cross and follow me.' He went on to say that if anyone wants to find their life, they must lose it. The call to discipleship is far more radical than the call to attend a church. The disciples we read about in the New Testament left everything to follow Christ. They gave their lives to learn from Him and act like Him.

The challenge that we have experienced, as we have transitioned from the old to the new, has been that many Christians are finding Jesus' words to be too demanding. The 24/7 call of Christ upon their lives, money and time is challenging. But this is the heart of being a disciple. It is not for a particular day or hour of the week, but for a person's whole life. As Master and Lord, and the one who gave up His life for us, Jesus claims exclusive ownership over everything, which is why He can speak these strong words.

How Can We Reproduce Disciples?

Making disciples is a strong part of *being* a disciple. In the old wineskin, the main way of trying to bring people into the Kingdom was to get them to come to church on a Sunday, hear a sermon by the preacher, and maybe they would walk to the front when an altar call was given and pray a prayer. The difference with disciple-making is that the responsibility of salvation rests with every follower of Christ - no longer getting someone to church but instead *being* the Church.

The command in Matthew 28 was given not only to the Early Church leaders but also to every disciple. The aim then becomes to mobilise the whole body of Christ to be sharing their faith, leading people to Christ and teaching them to obey Christ. The end goal is not to get a person to pray a prayer but to become more like Jesus as they study His word and spend time with Him for themselves. Yes, large gatherings will play a role in this, but they are not the only or the primary way in which disciples are made. Paul instructed, in 1 Corinthians 11:1, to 'Follow my example, as I follow the example of Christ.' We should all have people in our lives whom we seek to imitate and people in our lives whom we are helping to form Christ in. In other words, we are all being discipled and discipling others.

In 2 Timothy 2:2, Paul says, 'And the things you have heard me say in the presence of many witnesses entrust to reliable people who will also be qualified to teach others.' In this one verse, Paul mentions four generations who will go on to make disciples. Paul taught Timothy, Timothy was instructed to teach others, and those others are told to teach others also. This is very important for us to understand. Disciple-making is reproductive and generational. You don't need to be an expert before you can start making disciples. In John 4, when Jesus meets the lady at the well, as soon as she realises that He is the Messiah, she goes out and tells others to come to Jesus. In the same way, in John 1 and 2, as Jesus calls disciples, they are already calling others to come and see the Messiah. You don't have to know everything, see everything or have been saved for a certain length of time. You just need to be in love with Jesus and be able to take other people to Him. We can all help others to step into their full potential in Christ.

Disciple-making will be a hallmark of the new that God is doing. As we become disciples who make disciples, we will see this become a viral, organic move that the Spirit blows through. We read in Acts that the

Early Church grew daily, with 3,000 being added to their number on the day of Pentecost alone (Acts 2:41).

Effective disciple-making leads to churches being planted. Jesus commanded us to make disciples and said that He would build His Church (Matthew 16:18). Instead, many leaders have been building the Church and have hoped that God would turn the people into disciples.

As a couple, we have sought to be more aware, when going about our normal life activities, of the people around us. Whether it's in the gym, going for a walk or doing the food shopping, we have started asking the Lord to help us notice those around us. In a hurried world, we must create space for people if we are to be making disciples. We have had the painful realisation that we were more aligned to the life of a convert than a disciple. This has led to repentance and asking the Lord for His grace to fully obey Jesus' Great Commission.

One way in which we have sought to make disciples is by embracing smaller missional communities, or home churches. It is in smaller groups that are planted in neighbourhoods, as believers pray, study the Bible and do mission together in their localities, that we will see people becoming disciples of Christ. While we are not advocating a particular model for all churches, we would encourage every church leader to seriously consider whether the way they are doing church facilitates the making of disciples or whether it feeds the consumer culture.

What Now?

1. Make disciples. The call to make disciples is for every believer. Ask the Lord for help to obey the Great Commission and for eyes to see the world and the people around you as He does.

2. How can you create space in your life to invite people on to the journey? See the resources recommended in the section on disciple-making.

Prayer

Then Jesus came to them and said, 'All authority in heaven and on earth has been given to me. Therefore, go and make disciples of all nations, baptising them in the name of the Father and of the Son and of the Holy Spirit, and teaching them to obey everything I have commanded you. And surely, I am with you always, to the very end of the age.'
- **Matthew 28:18-20**

Lord, I have been guilty of living with a Sunday-Christianity mindset and have neglected the Great Commission. I have not always seen the people around me as potential disciples. Please would You forgive me and grant me Your perspective? I recommit myself to obeying the Great Commission. Would You help me to become a disciple who makes disciples? I submit to Your Lordship and leadership in my life.
Amen

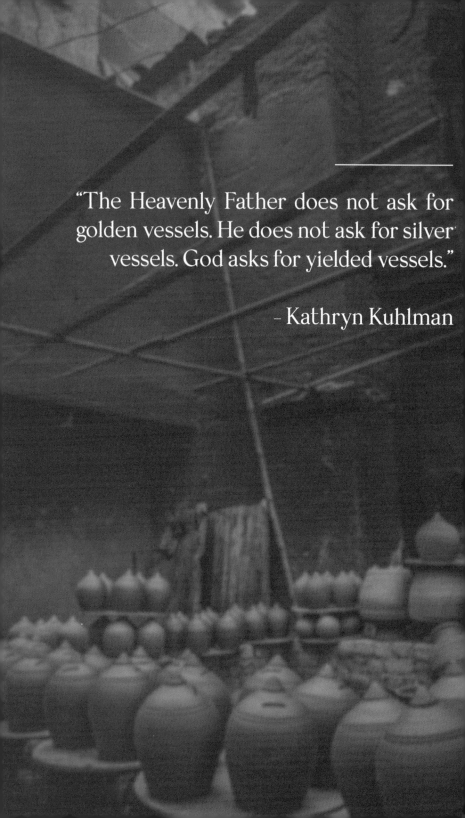

"The Heavenly Father does not ask for golden vessels. He does not ask for silver vessels. God asks for yielded vessels."

- Kathryn Kuhlman

CHAPTER 15 -
OBEDIENCE, OBEDIENCE, OBEDIENCE

O ne of the key hallmarks of a disciple of Christ is radical obedience. We touched on this very briefly in a previous chapter but want to expound it here more fully. At the beginning of our journey into the new, we felt the Lord challenge us that we were measuring ourselves by what others were doing and not by what the Lord was asking of us. One of the key passages that was highlighted to us was the Great Commission in Matthew 28. As we shared in the previous chapter, we had convinced ourselves that seeing converts on a Sunday was the same thing as making disciples.

There is also a tendency in the current church culture to compromise biblical truth for a socially acceptable and palatable message. This is both sad and very dangerous. The Church was never meant to fit in with the world. If the Church does not stand to her full height and fill her place in society, this creates a vacuum that the enemy will occupy. Our personal conviction is that, owing to the diminishing stature of the Church, we are witnessing a degrading in the culture around us.

It is easy to confuse familiarity with the commands of God as obedience to them. Hearing and believing the teachings of Jesus is important, but it must lead to obedience. We see this comparison drawn in the parable of the wise and foolish builders in Matthew 7:24-27. There has never been a generation that has as much knowledge available as we do today. We have easy access to Bibles in countless translations, audiobooks, sermons, worship sets, conferences and the internet to search things out. It is clear from Luke 12:48 that, 'From everyone who has been given much, much will be demanded.' 'Knowledge puffs up while love builds up' (1 Corinthians 8:1). We don't want to become a knowledgeable people who fail to act. We must be faithful with the much that has been given to us by responding in obedience.

We are to obey the Lord because we love Him. In John 14:15, Jesus says that our obedience is a sign of our love. Our primary motivation in obeying is not legalism and duty, but a love relationship with the Father. As we recognise all that He has done for us, and the obedience of Jesus to death on a cross, we ought to respond with the same willingness to obey. In John 15:10, Jesus says that just as He obeyed the Father to remain in His love, so we are to obey Him if we are to remain in His love. If Jesus obeyed His Father, then, as His disciples being transformed into His likeness, we are called to the same level of obedience.

We obey because we belong to a Kingdom with a loving and good King. Unlike in a democracy, we don't get an opinion on whether to implement the King's commands. He has given us a way of life and a Kingdom value system designed to cultivate human flourishing. If we say Jesus is our King, then our lives should come into alignment with His leadership.

We obey because faith looks like something; it takes action. We read in the Old Testament about Abraham's obedience when he was instructed to sacrifice his son Isaac (Genesis 22). He was willing to obey, even though it seemed to fly in the face of everything he understood about God and His promises. Abraham was convinced that the Lord was good and faithful, that He knew best and could be trusted. Therefore, he willingly obeyed at great personal cost. Our lives should be filled with faith actions, small and big. Forgiving, loving, turning the other cheek, giving extravagantly, sharing Christ with others and much more are all steps of faith-filled obedience.

Finally, we obey because the Lord expects it of us. At the end of our lives, when we stand before Christ, we will not be judged by how good we were compared to other Christians. We will not be measured by our own views of what was right or wrong. The Lord has already given us His unchanging standard on life, godliness, sexuality, the way to live and much more. We will each give an account of our obedience or disobedience to what the Lord reveals in Scripture and the way He has asked us to respond and live.

This realisation has been a real personal challenge to us over the past two years as we have at times felt the temptation to go back to the way things were before. Yet we cannot deny that, through the scriptures that have been highlighted and the prophetic words given, the Lord has spoken ever so clearly. Therefore, we have no option but to obey. Living in the light of eternity and with a sense of the fear of God has been a big motivator. We want to make sure we hear the words, 'Well done, good and faithful servant' (Matthew 25:21).

Though we have talked about obedience being based in love, the fear of God and the love of God are different sides of the same coin. And both are working in our lives to produce obedience to the King.

But the eyes of the LORD are on those *who fear him,*
on those whose hope is in his *unfailing love,*
- **Psalm 33:18**

We must redefine what it means to be successful in the Lord's eyes and celebrate faithful obedience over short-term results. We can share the gospel with people, but it is the Lord who leads a sinner's heart to repentance. We can pray for someone who is sick, but it is the Lord who can bring about healing. Yes, we contend for fullness in all areas and for greater fruit, but we must understand that obedience is what the Father seeks.

Just after Jesus left the Earth, there were only 120 people in the upper room. It may be tempting to think that these results weren't great. In His final years on Earth, Jesus had seen crowds of thousands gather to hear His messages and whole villages running out to mountainsides to have their sick healed. Nevertheless, Jesus was obedient to what the Father called Him to do, and His life was a success. We can take encouragement from the fact that our success is not counted in numbers but in obedience.

Jesus isn't looking for a people who simply agree with His teaching, but for a people who will follow Him with utter abandonment and radical, wholehearted obedience. Disobedience, although often subtle, has been prevalent in the lives of many professing Christians. This needs to change if we are to be revival ready and are to embrace the new of what God has for us and what He is unfolding in our times. Obedience shuts the door to the enemy but disobedience can open doors to the enemy (Genesis 4:7).

What Now?

1. Ask the Holy Spirit to show you where you have been living with disobedience in your life, then repent of it. This may be revealed as you read through Scripture or share with others, or it may just come through an inner conviction.

2. Decide to obey quickly when the Lord shows you something you ought to be doing. Remember that the reward is in the obedience and not in the outcome.

Prayer

If you love me, keep my commands.
- John 14:15

Father, thank You that You love me and call me to a life of obedience. Help me to live in Your love and to obey Your commands. Give me an eternal perspective and help me not simply to measure my life by the standards of those around me.
Amen

Part IV: Posture

S it up straight.' 'Don't slouch.' 'Bend your knees when lifting.' These are all phrases we have said to our children over the years to keep them from suffering the consequences of poor posture. Incorrect posture can cause a person pain, affect their mobility and, in the long run, even cause deformity. Correct posture, on the other hand, helps keep a person agile, flexible and moving freely without pain.

'Posture' simply means the position in which someone holds themselves. It can refer to our attitudes, demeanour and lifestyle. Many of God's people have been suffering with bad posture. Whether it is attitudes of pride, self-sufficiency or unforgiveness, these things can lead to distorted perspective, reduced mobility and pain. If we want to be able to move into all that God has for us and truly be revival ready, we must become a people who are correctly positioned and aligned. We must adjust our attitudes and thinking to His ways and position ourselves so that we see from His perspective. From this corrected posture, we will again begin to walk in sustained power and authority in a way that allows for free movement of the Holy Spirit.

The next few chapters will look at some of the non-negotiable characteristics (or postures) for the emerging end-time generation. This next chapter complements abiding in Christ that we have already explored and provides a further way to go deeper.

"Let us fix our eyes on Jesus,
the author and perfecter of our faith"

- Hebrews 12:2

CHAPTER 16 - FIX YOUR EYES ON JESUS

When learning to drive, we are frequently told to keep our eyes on the road ahead. Why? Because a person will eventually end up in the place where they are looking. In the same way, the writer of the letter to the Hebrews, when encouraging believers to run their race well, says that our eyes ought to be fixed on Jesus (Hebrews 12:2). The eyes may not initially seem to be an important body part during a race, but without them we would not know which direction to go in. Just as when driving we must keep our eyes on the road to avoid veering off on to the kerb, unless we keep our eyes on Jesus, we run the risk of veering off and causing damage. Where we fix our eyes is an important part of a healthy overall posture.

Where we fix our eyes determines the affections of our heart. Jesus Himself said, in Luke 12:34, 'Where your treasure is, there your heart will be also.' It can be tempting to think that it is the other way around, that our hearts will lead our treasure, but where we put our money, time and focus is where our heart will go.

There has always been opportunity for distraction, but it has perhaps never been more pronounced than it is right now. Whether it is notifications popping up on our phone, the bombardment of social media or the pull of entertainment and materialism, it can seem as if there are a thousand other voices competing for our attention and affection.

The Lord knows that we are surrounded by potential distractions, and because of this there are countless commands in the Bible to 'pay attention' to what God is saying. We would love to list many of them, but here are two that have been very poignant for us.

My son, pay attention to what I say;

turn your ear to my words.

- Proverbs 4:20

We must pay the most careful attention, therefore, to what we have heard, so that we do not drift away.

- Hebrews 2:1

Learning to bring our attention constantly back to Christ is perhaps one of the most challenging, and yet necessary, things we can do. Colossians 3:1-2 commands us to 'set [our] minds on things above'. Fixing our eyes on Jesus is another way of obeying the command of Jesus in John 15 to abide in Him. We must learn to lift our eyes and live from heaven's reality. Men and women who have effected change in their generation have always been anchored in another realm.

As well as the distractions that come from outside the Church, there has been a temptation to get distracted with the demands of ministry. The Church has also allowed the world's value system to slip in, and we see this in the celebrity culture across the Church globally, whether preachers, pastors or worship leaders. This also distracts us by taking our eyes of Jesus and putting them on His servants. But there is a shift taking place.

See, I am doing a new thing!

Now it springs up; do you not perceive it?

I am making a way in the wilderness

and streams in the wasteland.

- Isaiah 43:19

If we are to be ready for the fresh outpouring of God's Spirit, we must see that He is doing a new thing and accept the fact that our old structures are no longer fit for purpose. As long as we stay focused on (and distracted by) our strategies, budgets and buildings, we will not see the societal transformation that is needed and promised. It is dangerous to become big in our own small bubble and not realise that we are not meeting the real need of the hour. It is easy to judge by exterior impressions and outward appearances, but we must have eyes to see what the Lord is showing. In 1 Samuel 16:7, the Lord says to Samuel that He does not look at the outward appearance, as people do, but ultimately He looks at the heart.

Don't get us wrong, we love the Church and appreciate what she is currently doing to advance the Kingdom of God. But what has served a purpose in one season will not necessarily work for the next. We must reposition our focus and realign our gaze if we are to step into all that God has.

We thought that this would be a relevant place to share a dream that Esther had back in 2016:

> I was in a theatre and on the stage were stood the full cast of a show. They came together, held hands, stepped forward and took their final bow. The theatre was packed out and those watching were applauding. I observed the actors step back and part, ready for the star of the show to make his final entrance. As he did, the theatre erupted with cheering and shouting. He had a standing ovation. The atmosphere was electric.
>
> When I awoke from the dream, I heard the words 'Act two, Scene two'. I instinctively knew I must read Acts chapter 2 and felt the significance of Acts 2 as the second half of the story.

We felt that the actors in this dream represent the Church. We must come together, hand in hand, and stand together in unity. Taking a bow speaks of a posture of humility, which is a vital key to a move of God's Spirit. We know that the Lord resists the proud but gives grace to the humble (James 4:6). Just as the actors moved aside to make room for the star of the show, the Church must get out of the way to make room for Jesus. We believe the audience in the dream represents the 'great cloud of witnesses' described in Hebrews 12:1. They surround us and are cheering us on in our race.

Just as in this dream there was a shift away from the actors to the star character, we believe that this shift is also taking place in the Church. There is only one star of the show. His name is Jesus. He will not share His glory with another, and we must prepare the way for Him. The Lord is graciously calling a distracted, busy people to fix our eyes on Him once again. Jesus is coming front and centre to His Church and will not allow anyone else to have the place reserved only for Him.

> Not to us, LORD, not to us
> but to your name be the glory,
> because of your love and faithfulness.
> - **Psalm 115:1**

What Now?

It takes constant and daily readjustments to fix our eyes on Jesus. Below are a few practical ideas for how you could do this throughout a day:

1. There is power in coming to the Lord early in the morning (Psalm 5:3). When you wake up, rather than responding to emails, checking the news or scrolling through social media, start the day by looking to Jesus. You can do this by reading the Bible and spending time in prayer and worship.

2. Pray with others throughout a day. We have found that both as a couple and as a family, praying together in the middle of conversations is a great way of acknowledging that the Lord is with us. Ask the Holy Spirit for promptings and reminders to pray with others.

3. Pray 30-40 ten-second prayers throughout a day as a way of constantly turning your heart towards Him.

- Lord, I love You. Help me to know Your love.

- Lord, what are You thinking? What are You feeling?

- Lord, increase my awareness of You right now.

4. At the end of a day, take a moment to journal and process the day with the Lord. You might choose to do this with your family around the evening meal.

Prayer

… fixing our eyes on Jesus, the pioneer and perfecter of faith. For the joy that was set before him he endured the cross, scorning its shame, and sat down at the right hand of the throne of God.
- **Hebrews 12:2**

Lord, would You help me to keep my eyes fixed on You? In the midst of all the distractions and busyness, I need Your help to remember that You are the star of the show. I want to run the race that You have mapped out for me and not veer off to the right or to the left. Please, keep me on the right path.
Amen

"The greatness of a man's power is
the measure of his surrender. "

– William Booth

CHAPTER 17 - GO LOW

The phrase 'go low' is part of a larger phrase the Lord spoke to us a few years ago: 'Go low, go slow, don't put on a show.' This phrase kept coming back to us in our times of prayer.

To go low is to be humble. Humility is one of the key characteristics for all who call themselves followers of Jesus and it is a necessary posture to enter the new. As we began to make certain adjustments early in the journey, we found that other church leaders were asking us to share what we were doing and why. There was a curiosity among a variety of denominations as to what the new involved. Though there was a real temptation to give clever answers and appear as though we knew exactly what we were doing, we felt the warning of the Holy Spirit to stay in the place of humility. We shared some of the revelations but found ourselves saying to people to come back and ask the questions in two to four years when we might know more of what God was saying. That is still our answer today. We are learning to hear God and we do not see the full picture but are convinced that humility is a key pathway to staying true.

There is a bias in the human heart to put our best foot forward. Whether it is through social media or writing books, we want to give the impression that we know what we are doing and that we are doing it well. This is as true in the Church as it is outside it. There can also be a tendency to downplay the severity of pride, especially in today's culture, but pride is extremely offensive to the Lord. Pride and arrogance have become acceptable and even celebrated in the Church. This is seen in self-promotion and bragging about our achievements, but we must not allow that deception to become acceptable to us. We must understand that pride is extremely dangerous and must be avoided at all cost. God hates and detests pride:

> To fear the LORD is to hate evil;
>
> I hate pride and arrogance,
>
> evil behaviour and perverse speech.
>
> **- Proverbs 8:13**

> The LORD detests all the proud of heart.
>
> Be sure of this: they will not go unpunished.
>
> **- Proverbs 16:5**

We do not want the Lord to actively resist us. Yet this is what He does if we become proud (James 4:6). The opposite is also true: God gives grace to the humble (James 4:6). Francis Frangipane says that 'humility is the door opener to grace; no virtue enters our lives except that humility requests it come'.[6] We need His grace if we are to enter the new of what He has for us.

The Bible is full of promises and rewards for humility as well as warnings against pride. There is not sufficient space in this chapter to go through each of these in detail, but we would encourage you to look at the resources on the subject of humility in the Further Reading section.

---

[6] Francis Frangipane, in a sermon preached in 2005. Used with permission. www.frangipane.org

Ultimately, we are to walk in humility because this is how Jesus walked. Whether it was leaving heaven to become a baby in a manger, washing the feet of His disciples or dying the death of a criminal, at every stage of His life, Jesus took the lowly path. As we seek to be His disciples, our lives ought to look like His life. When we choose to go low, we choose the way of the Saviour. This is also the way recognised and honoured by our heavenly Father.

In John 7:3-4, Jesus' brothers try to persuade Jesus to go to the festival. They tell Him that it is a what a 'public figure' should do and that He should 'show [Himself] to the world'. Jesus is not persuaded or moved by their argument of how people should do things. Rather, Jesus displays humility by waiting for the leading of His Father. There may be many voices, even familiar voices, in your life telling you that you must behave a certain way. Even the example set by other Christians can pressurise us to give in to a worldly, proud way of living. Yet we must not go the popular way. We must choose the correct way and go low.

The very nature of something being 'new' means that we do not yet understand it all. Walking in humility keeps us teachable. One of our friends, Sharon Stone, has said, 'I would rather be a novice in the new than an expert in the old.' With humility comes wisdom, and we need wisdom to step into the new.

Transition of Authority and Power

In Isaiah 22:20-22, we see a transition of authority and power taking place. The Lord is removing a man named Shebna and replacing him with another man named Eliakim. Shebna has been building for himself, has been protecting his own image and is proud and arrogant. The Lord is harsh in His rebuke and says He will throw him off like a coat. Eliakim, on the other hand, is chosen to replace Shebna because he will be a father and a servant.

Just as there was a transition of power in Isaiah 22, we believe there is a transition of power taking place right now in the global Church. The Lord is moving certain people out of the way, those who have sought to build their own empires and who have looked to themselves. He is replacing them with people of humility who will be spiritual fathers and mothers and who will be servant-hearted. There is a transition happening in the Kingdom and in the Church from rulers and leaders to fathers and mothers. Leaders raise up followers, but fathers and mothers raise up sons and daughters. We will see the rise of some people who are currently unknown and the demise of those that we once looked up to but who have become self-sufficient, self-protecting and self-promoting.

This transition is taking place because the Lord is preparing the Church for the coming season. Just as He gave Shebna time to change, He has been gracious with his Church. But Proverbs 29:1 warns that if a person remains stiff-necked after many rebukes, they will suddenly be broken. Unless we respond by posturing ourselves in humility, we may find that we are moved to one side and are broken beyond repair. A tender heart and asking the Lord to help us is really important. Praying with others and asking them to hold us accountable is also a really good way of aligning ourselves to what the Lord is doing.

~

Below is a picture that Esther had back in May 2021 which we felt was a relevant way to conclude this chapter:

> I hear the sound of the wind in the trees, firmly rooted and yet bending as the wind blows. The wind of the Spirit is blowing, and we must be flexible. I hear the Lord saying, 'Can you hear the sound?' It's the sound of the new wineskins. He is raising new-wineskin people, people who are able to bend, people of humility, flexibility and capacity. God is raising wise and humble leaders who will give all the glory to God.

C J Mahaney in his book *Humility* encourages us to look daily for ways to weaken pride and to cultivate humility.[7] This really is a daily and lifelong journey that we must embrace.

What Now?

1. Practise gratitude. Take time every day to thank the Lord for the things He has given to you. When we live with a sense of gratitude, we remain humble.

2. Acknowledge your dependence on the Lord in the way you pray to Him.

---

[7] C J Mahaney, *Humility: True Greatness* (Colorado Springs: Multnomah Books, 2005), p. 169.

3. Look for ways to serve others each day, both in small ways and in more costly ways.

4. We can weaken pride as we reflect on the cross. How can anyone be arrogant when they stand at the foot of the cross? Perhaps set aside a regular, even daily, time to break bread and remember what God has done. This could be over a meal with your household or in a small group setting.

Prayer

> Search me, God, and know my heart;
> test me and know my anxious thoughts.
> See if there is any offensive way in me,
> and lead me in the way everlasting.
> **- Psalm 139:23-24**

Lord, I recognise my great need of You. I can do nothing without You. Would You help me to walk as Jesus did, in a posture of humility, as I enter the new of what You are doing. Remove pride from my life; help me to break out of the mindset of popular culture that teaches us to elevate self.
Amen

_____

"Going slow at the beginning gives
us the ability to go faster later."

- Esther Uppal

CHAPTER 18 - GO SLOW

We have looked at what it means to 'go low', and now we will look at the importance of 'going slow'. Over the last two years, as we have been receiving revelation from the Lord, there has been a real sense of excitement. We felt as though we just wanted to run with all that the Lord was saying. There was a temptation to move quickly into what we were beginning to see. Though there are times when the Spirit moves at a fast pace, there are other moments when it feels as though He slows us down. This journey was one that we felt needed to be taken slowly. The Lord was not simply changing a model or a programme; He was changing us. He was changing the way we thought, the way we processed things and the way our teams operated. In hindsight, if we had moved too quickly, we would have made many mistakes. We had to fight our cultural mindset to seize the moment, take control and build the Church!

In the spring of 2020, through different times in prayer, we kept hearing the Lord impress upon us that we needed to give two years to turn the 'ship' around and then a further three years to establish the new patterns and rhythms and allow the roots to go deep. Though we heard this time frame and knew it was the Lord speaking, there was a part of us that felt as though we could make the change much more quickly. But now, being a couple of years into the process, we see the wisdom in the Lord's time frame and are learning to embrace His speed. The shift is so big that we need to give it time and to pace ourselves. The going slow allows us to do this and to build the endurance needed. We believe if we go slow at the beginning, it will enable us to go faster later.

One of our leadership team had a picture, early on, of a person walking through a clear stream slowly and carefully so as not to muddy the water. We interpreted this to mean that if we wanted sustained clarity, we needed to tread carefully into all that God had for us.

Sadly, many have forgotten what it is to be led by the Spirit and to keep in step with Him (Galatians 5:25). Yet, 'those who are led by the Spirit of God are the children of God' (Romans 8:14). Some would rather read a book, attend a conference and follow a set of prescribed steps than go directly to the Saviour. While God can and does use these things to help us – and we hope that He uses this book to do so too – other sources must not replace our ability to hear from God for ourselves. Often, the speed at which we live stops us being able to hear and see what God is saying and doing. When we slow down and take time to be still, then we begin to hear the voice of the Lord.

In reading through the book of Acts, or looking at the life of Jesus and the Apostle Paul, we see what it means to be led by the Spirit. In John 3:8, Jesus talks about those who are born of the Spirit being like the wind: 'You hear its sound, but you cannot tell where it comes from or where it is going.' Just as the wind is unpredictable, for those of us who are born of the Spirit, our lives and timelines will be unpredictable. There will be days when we hear the Lord telling us to do one thing, and days He says to do another. Part of the new that the Lord is ushering in is to help the Church to live led by the Spirit again. Change takes time.

In Acts 13:2, we see the believers coming together to worship and fast. As they are doing so, the Holy Spirit leads them to send out Barnabas and Paul. There is something powerful about extended times of prayer, worship and fasting together with other believers. They lead to wisdom about decisions that need making. In our experience, it is rare to find church leaders spending a day or two regularly praying and fasting together. We believe that the Lord wants to restore this to His Church. At the beginning of 2022, we decided to introduce a day at the beginning of our Fuel the Fire leaders' event, to gather with other leaders in the city and to fast and pray. We have now done this up and down the country with groups of leaders and in numerous churches. These have been powerful times of prayer and listening, and a number of leaders have been encouraged to implement this with their teams.

Living from Listening

We have been challenged to live and lead from listening. It's easy to live from habit or the demands placed upon us by others but real fruitfulness flows from listening to the Lord. Jesus Himself said that He only did what He saw the Father doing (John 5:19).

So how do we know what pace to keep? By living led by the Spirit. While this application may sound a little mystical, the Lord is developing the spiritual ear of the Church and delivering us from a strategy-driven mindset. We're not against strategy or leadership principles, but these must come into submission to the Bible and the Spirit. We serve a speaking God and we must be a listening people. The Lord will not only tell us what to do but He will also tell us when to do it.

~

Below is a dream that Esther had in April 2021. We felt this was relevant to include here as it highlights some of the dangers of rushing into what God has.

Steve and I were on holiday with Sophia, Joel and Judah (three of our children). We were on the beach and the boys could not wait to get into the sea. Joel kept asking to go into the surf. Steve was reluctant and said it was a bit early in the day. I said they could go to the edge but only ankle deep. Sophia would not go with them.

After only moments I felt an urgency to go and check on them. There were huge waves and sand could only be seen briefly for a moment when the waves withdrew. They were already in over their heads. Other children were in the sea too. Joel had a surfboard but could not control it. It was being spun by every wave. Alarmed, and now looking for Judah, I climbed higher to find him. Steve was behind me and I shouted that we must get them out of the water. I could not see Judah at all and waited for the next wave to withdraw, only to see him lifeless on the sand.

This was my moment. I had to act quickly and wasted no time sprinting to where he was. Somehow, I had the strength to carry him to safety. He was actually younger-looking now, like a toddler. I lay him down and began CPR. It worked and water gushed out of his mouth as he gasped for air. I picked him up and held him close. I awoke with my heart racing, full of emotion.

In dreams, people can represent different things and names can often be significant. As the children were growing up, there were numerous words spoken by different people about the God-given calling on their lives. Joel, we believe, is a reference to the prophetic, because of the prophet Joel. Judah, we believe, represents the apostolic. Sophia means 'wisdom', and we believe she represents the wisdom of God in this dream.

Revival, like the waves in this dream, is coming and is about to break upon our shores. The prophetic and the apostolic, like Joel and Judah in the dream, can see it, they are excited and want to rush out into the waves. The senior apostolic voice, represented by Steve, warns that it is premature, but many who are younger in their gifts do not pay attention. Wisdom, represented by Sophia, was also holding back. We must pay attention to the wisdom and warnings of God and wait for His timing.

What God is about to do on the Earth is awesome, and He is to be feared, just like these waves. We must approach what comes next with radical obedience and caution, and not just excitement. The waves are powerful and could destroy us if we do not wait for the right time. We must climb higher to get clarity and to rescue those who may have rushed out too soon. We must stay in step with the Spirit. We need the Word of God, the Spirit of God and the people of God. We must learn to hold steady and to submit to one another. We need each other, not only to discover destiny but also to reach our destination at the right time.

What Now?

1. Set aside some time to pray and fast with other believers. This is a great way of hearing the Holy Spirit as we read about in Acts.

2. Are there any practical things you can do to slow your pace of life?

3. Being led by the Spirit is relevant not just to the big decisions, but also to the small decisions we make each and every day. Practise hearing God in the small decisions by asking for His leading as you go about your day-to-day life.

Prayer

Since we live by the Spirit, let us keep in step with the Spirit.
- **Galatians 5:25**

Lord, would You help me to keep step with You? I don't want to run ahead and I don't want to drag behind. Help me to be patient and to wait for Your timing in everything.
Amen

———————

"It is only the fear of God, that can deliver us from the fear of man."

- John Witherspoon

CHAPTER 19 - DON'T PUT ON A SHOW

The third aspect to the phrase, we felt, is, 'Don't put on a show.' This idea is closely linked with going low and the importance of humility. This chapter will only be brief, but we felt it is still important to make the distinction.

Comparing oneself with others and how we believe they perceive us is a major challenge throughout the world. Social media, and the immediacy of seeing photos and videos of what others are doing, has created an unhealthy comparison where individuals view their own lives by the highlight reels of what others post. When individuals, couples, families, businesses and even churches compare themselves in this way, it can breed competition. It can also pressure us to take paths that are not within the Lord's leading for us. Much of this is not verbalised. It takes place in the hearts, thoughts and emotions of individuals.

This is as true in the Church as it is outside it, whether it's the comparison of worship styles trending on YouTube or Spotify, or the comparison between different speakers and their approach to delivering sermons. Covid-19 didn't particularly help with this, as many turned to online services and were faced with a menu of options allowing them to pick exactly what they fancied at a particular time.

Having travelled to lots of different places and preached in different churches and contexts, we have felt the comparison game on a personal level. Upon meeting new leaders, we have often been asked questions about the size of our building and congregation, the number of books we have written or our social media following. All these questions, though innocent in themselves, are all part of a person trying to gauge how 'successful' we may be. We have also fallen into that trap! All of us want to be perceived well by others and there is a temptation to promote self. Self-promotion is not the way of the Kingdom, and it flies in the face of New Testament Christianity.

If we are to move into all that the Lord has for us, we must be free from comparison, competition and self-promotion. No one can obey the Lord fully while being concerned about how they are perceived by others. Men and women who have changed the world throughout history have cared little about what others have thought of them but have given themselves to faithfully obeying the Lord.

When we root ourselves in the love of God, the pressure of what others are doing loses its grip. We are not to be replicas of each other but are to embrace the uniqueness that the Father calls each of us into.

We believe God is raising a Church that will walk in humility, in unity and in response to what the Father is saying, rather than in response to what others are doing. We must cut off the spirit of comparison and competition, otherwise we will be pushed or pulled out of the will of God.

We would strongly urge you to embrace meekness, which is power under control. Meekness chooses not to flaunt one's gifts, achievements, money or status, but intentionally chooses a lowly path and serves others. Meek people walk differently, talk differently and see the best in others.

What Now?

1. Ask a trusted Christian friend to help you see how competition has taken root and pray with them; invite them to challenge you whenever they see it in you.

2. List practical changes you can make to weaken the hold of comparison, and then pray for grace to follow through.

3. Ask the Holy Spirit for His help to live rooted in the Father's love and free from comparison.

Prayer

You are still worldly. For since there is jealousy and quarrelling among you, are you not worldly? Are you not acting like mere humans?

- 1 Corinthians 3:3

Father, please deliver me from being worldly when I have lived with comparison and jealousy. Help me to walk in the freedom You provide. Set me free from the fear of what others think and root me deeply into Your love.

Amen

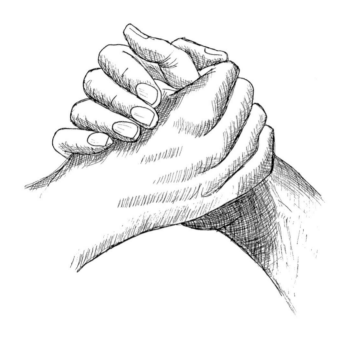

Part V: People

In the Old Testament, God's dwelling place was first the Tabernacle and then the Temple. But under the New Covenant, He lives in His people. This is a glorious mystery and was God's eternal plan (Colossians 1:27). Rediscovering the glory and beauty of God living in and through His people is more significant than many realise. Some of us may have a correct theology of the priesthood of *all* believers yet do not experience it being lived out in practice. We believe that the Lord Himself is mobilising His whole body, the Church. The next and perhaps the final move of God that brings in the promised great harvest of souls will be marked by a release of His people rising up to their full potential.

"We are created by community, fashioned for fellowship and formed for a family and none of us can fulfil God's purposes by ourselves."

- Rick Warren

CHAPTER 20 - KINGDOM COMMUNITY

A s mentioned in previous chapters, the new wineskin does not refer primarily to organisational structures, but to the people who make up those structures. We belong to a relational Kingdom; this has been highlighted to us again in the current season. The primary strategy of heaven is relationship, and the Kingdom of God moves at the speed of relationship.

Created for Relationship with God

Right at the beginning of time, in the Garden of Eden, we see that God intended to have friendship with humans (Genesis 3:8). He walked with them and talked with them. When this relationship was damaged because of sin, we see the storyline of a loving Father unfold as He goes to extraordinary lengths to restore the relationship – ultimately sending Jesus to die.

One of the primary revelations Jesus brings is of God as 'Father'. He refers to God in this way more than a hundred times in the Gospel of John alone. This would have been revolutionary for the Jewish people, who held God in reverence and at a distance but never knew Him in such an intimate way. Yet everything comes back to this ultimate and primary relationship. When describing eternal life, Jesus says, eternal life is *knowing* the Father and the Son (John 17:3). This relational aspect of the Kingdom to which we belong is foundational. Getting this correct is essential to enable the building of healthy relationships, ministries and churches.

Created for Relationship with Each Other

Not only are we created for relationship with our heavenly Father, but we are also commanded to live in close relationship with one other. In fact, from the relationship and joining we have with the Father will spring the true relational joining we have with His body. Interestingly, the invitation of Jesus, in countless New Testament passages, is not to read a certain set of rules, nor to follow a particular code of conduct, nor to meet in a particular venue at a set time. The invitation of Jesus is always to 'come and follow' Him (Matthew 4:19, John 1:35-39). These simple but compelling words reveal His desire for relationship.

> Jesus said to him, "'You shall love the Lord your God with all your heart, with all your soul, and with all your mind.' This is the first and great commandment. And the second is like it: 'You shall love your neighbor as yourself.' On these two commandments hang all the Law and the Prophets."
> **- Matthew 22:37-40**

When Jesus was asked about the greatest commandment, He essentially summed it up as: love God, love people. This is more important and challenging than many of us may at first realise. To love God with *all* one's heart, soul and mind is not an easy or a quick thing. It is a lifelong pursuit. It is only as we learn to love God, that it becomes possible to love others as we love ourselves – the first commandment empowers us to obey the second. In one of His final prayers on Earth, Jesus interceded for the unity of all believers that they may be one as He and the Father were one. Jesus' prayer will be answered, and we may well be the answer in our lifetime as we step into unity with other believers.

> I do not pray for these alone, but also for those who will believe in Me through their word; that they all may be one, as You, Father, are in Me, and I in You; that they also may be one in Us, that the world may believe that You sent Me. And the glory which You gave Me I have given them, that they may be one just as We are one: I in them, and You in Me; that they may be made perfect in one, and that the world may know that You have sent Me, and have loved them as You have loved Me.
> - **John 17:20-23**

It is abundantly clear from these passages of Scripture that God's heart for His Church and His people has always been true community. The challenge, then, is to look at ourselves honestly and to ask whether this has been our priority. As we examine what much of the Church is currently doing, the way we spend our time and money, it seems as though the priority has been buildings, strategies and programmes.

We seem to have lost the simplicity and friendship that Jesus modelled in His invitation to follow Him. We have had to reluctantly acknowledge how easy it is for people to attend a Sunday service without engaging with others or building true relationships.

But God is bringing a shift away from organisational structures to relational ones. In these last days, we believe we will once again see the whole body, joined and held together by every supporting ligament, grow[ing] and build[ing] itself up in love, as each part does its work' (Ephesians 4:16). The Apostle Peter tells the believers that Christ is the living Stone and that we, like Him, are living stones that are being built into a spiritual house (1 Peter 2:4-5). Living people, joined to one another in relationship by His Spirit, become the dwelling place for a living God. This is the Lord's design, to dwell in his people collectively not just individually. We have become accustomed to witnessing and even expecting power from those on a platform, but we are about to see His whole house become a dwelling place for Him – every believer! This is where the power and fruitfulness of the Early Church came from. The Church will again be a beautiful, life-giving organism that is relationally joined – growing, maturing and advancing the Kingdom. This is not a passive, 'nice' group of people but a true community, full of the Spirit's life, power and authority. These will bring the needed transformation to our communities, cities and nations.

At least in our experience we have not yet seen true New Testament *koinonia*[8] as demonstrated in the book of Acts. It is a work of the Holy Spirit, and it is also a work God does through His apostles that helps form authentic Kingdom communities. We believe this will lead to a restoration of authority and power in those churches. We will explore this a little further in the forthcoming chapters on the Apostolic.

---

[8] Intimate Christian fellowship that is a work of the Spirit, resulting in the life of the Spirit in that group of people.

What Now?

Be completely humble and gentle; be patient, bearing with one another in love. Make every effort to keep the unity of the Spirit through the bond of peace.
- Ephesians 4:2-3

1. Ask the Holy Spirit for His help to keep the bond of peace with your fellow believers and to have His perspective on the body of Christ.

2. Think of a few practical ways you can commit to living more meaningfully in fellowship with other believers. We have called this a voluntary interdependence.

Prayer

My prayer is not for them alone. I pray also for those who will believe in me through their message, that all of them may be one, Father, just as you are in me and I am in you. May they also be in us so that the world may believe that you have sent me. I have given them the glory that you gave me, that they may be one as we are one.
- John 17:20-22

Thank You, Lord, that You are a relational God and that I belong to a relational Kingdom. Would You help me to get my priorities correct? I want to love You and others and choose to live in true Christian community. Would You help me to see the beauty and potential of Your body, the Church? Amen

"There are far better things ahead
then any we leave behind."

- C.S Lewis

CHAPTER 21 -
RESTORATION OF THE FIVEFOLD[9]

I n some contexts, using the term, 'apostle' or 'prophet' can be controversial. We have no desire to fuel controversy. We recognise that these, and other terms, have been abused by some over the years, bringing shame to the name of Christ. This happened in Paul's day, where some preached the gospel for selfish ambition and gain (Philippians 1:15-18). Notwithstanding the abuses, these roles, along with the rest of the fivefold, were given to the Church by Jesus Himself. They are gifts from the Lord to equip His people for service and to help bring them to maturity.

> So Christ himself gave the apostles, the prophets, the evangelists, the pastors and teachers, to equip his people for works of service, so that the body of Christ may be built up until we all reach unity in the faith and in the knowledge of the Son of God and become mature, attaining to the whole measure of the fullness of Christ.
>
> **- Ephesians 4:11-13**

---

[9] The term 'fivefold' refers to the five ministry gifts mentioned in Ephesians 4:11: 'So Christ himself gave the apostles, the prophets, the evangelists, the pastors and teachers.' While some see pastor and teacher as one gift, we are inclined to think they are distinct from each other. But the important thing is to recognise these gifts, which releases people to flourish in their callings.

The Lord has been highlighting to us the importance of the fivefold ministry working together and, in particular, the restoration of apostles and prophets. While we have seen expressions of these individual gifts across the Earth for quite some time, we are convinced that there will be a coming together and a sense of team that we have not yet seen.

A Brief Look at the Fivefold over Recent Decades[10]

In the 1950s, we saw the role of 'evangelist' being restored. There was a whole wave of tent meetings and stadium crusades. Powerful evangelist personalities took to the stage across the world – men like T L Osborn, Billy Graham and A A Allen, to mention just a few.

In the 1960s, we saw the role of 'pastor' being restored. Larger churches were emerging that were led by those who had strong pastoral gifts, and it became more common to use the term 'pastor' during this time.

In the 1970s, we saw the role of 'teacher' being restored. People like Derek Prince, Bob Mumford and many others rose up as powerful teachers. Many would go to their meetings, notepads in hand, and enjoy the anointing of the teacher.

In the 1980s, we saw the role of 'prophets' being restored. We saw waves of prophetic words, signs, wonders and declarations.

---

[10] John Alley's teachings have helped our understanding of this subject. https://www.peace.org.au/

Finally, in the 1990s, we started to see the emerging recognition of apostles in many countries. People like Terry Virgo, Bryn Jones, Gerald Coates and John Noble, to mention just a few, that began to emerge in the 1970s and build new streams and networks before there was a fresh wave of apostles in the 1990s. These and many others around the world were godly men who loved the Lord and pioneered a new way.

These roles clearly predate the past couple of decades; however, the way in which they emerged like this was fresh and new. Some people believed, at the end of that five-decade period, that the Church was fully restored. This was not the case. While we saw great things happen, there was a sense of independence and isolation in some of those ministries. Such independence creates a greater chance for error and for falling into sin. It also limits the true functionality of the Church. What we were missing was the fivefold coming together as a team. Only in team being restored can we reach maturity – we need each other. We are not in any way judging any of the ministries mentioned, but rather making a general point that the Church has yet to see the fivefold working together effectively.

Working Together as Family

God is bringing together the fivefold gifts in our day, in a way that will beautify the body of Christ. When these five become mutually committed to each other, submit to one another and defer to the strengths of the others, then the Church can truly become who she was always meant to be. Like diverse flowers in a hand-picked bouquet, these gifts will not clash but will bring out the best in one another and release a fragrance for His glory. Our hope is to see true team being restored as these five graces work in unity together.

Most people who attend church never really question who they are or the gifting they have been given. This has been one of the weaknesses of the old wineskin. As long as church members remain in this consumer mindset, the body of Christ will never fully mature. While not every believer is called to the office of one of the fivefold gifts – that is to say, they hold government and authority in a particular space – we believe that for every follower of Christ, there will be a primary and a secondary gifting in one of these five areas. For example, there may be those who have an evangelistic grace and find themselves expressing this within their own context. Some people are prophetic by nature while also having a grace for teaching. Others may find that they are pastoral in nature while also having a gift of evangelism.

Our interests, passions and strengths can all help to reveal to us the grace we have been given. As we are planted in community and surround ourselves with godly leaders, they can help us to identify who we are, what grace we carry and how to excel in that which we have. Just as fathers and mothers in the natural give identity to their children and help call out their destiny, in the same way, spiritual fathers and mothers help identity to be formed.

For those who sense a particular calling on their life, seeking fathers and mothers who will help them to grow and align in relationship is essential for the full mature development of the person and the grace given to them. If people don't know how to be a son or a daughter, they will never fully mature to become a father or a mother.

At a recent conference we hosted, we asked Brother Yun (the Heavenly Man),[11] 'With the thousands of home churches that you have throughout China, what qualities do you look for in your leaders?' His answer was surprising. He said, 'We don't have leaders. We have fathers and mothers.'

It was a powerful moment during a panel discussion as we realised that, in the West, we have a fascination with leaders. But in China, where the Church is growing so fast, they have a commitment to family. Even in speaking about the fivefold ministry, understanding the power of family and relationship and the true joining of the heart is essential – not only for us but also for the generations to come. This is not about organisational charts and who has more power or authority, but it really is the forming of true relational joining and family.

We believe the Lord is restoring families in both the natural and the spiritual. One of the last verses in the Old Testament tells us that, before the coming of the Lord, He 'will turn the hearts of the parents to their children, and the hearts of children to their parents' (Malachi 4:6). We believe that there will be a great restoration of true Christian community as we see a restoration of apostles, prophets, teachers, evangelists and pastors. Just as natural families are different, with each

---

[11] Brother Yun is the author of *The Heavenly Man: The Remarkable True Story of Chinese Christian Brother Yun* (Oxford: Monarch Books, 2002).

person having a unique character, personality and set of gifts, so will church families be different. No two leadership teams will look the same because each will be an expression of the Creator's magnificent originality. Rather than cookie-cutter replicas, God's plan is for each church and congregation to carry the identity of the people who form it.

What Now?

1. If you are not in one already, find a church community to be connected to. It is only in this context that we are able to fully mature and grow. We hear God better together.

2. Seek out spiritual mothers and fathers to help nurture the gift of God on your life.

3. Perhaps you have known dysfunction within your own family, whether natural or spiritual. Invite the Lord's help into these situations and believe that He is the God who can turn hearts.

Prayer

> But to each one of us grace has been given as Christ apportioned it. This is why it says: 'When he ascended on high, he took many captives and gave gifts to his people.'

- Ephesians 4:7-8

Father, I pray for a release of the gifts of the Spirit in the body of Christ. Lord, help us to see where we fit into Your big family. We want to know the graces that You have given to us and we want to play our part well. Remove any spirit of independence or competition. Help us to work together to build up the bride of Christ and to see Your Kingdom manifest on the Earth.

Amen

"Christ has never stopped building His church and He has never ceased gifting the church with apostles and prophets."

- T L Lowery

CHAPTER 22 -

FOUNDATION OF APOSTLES AND PROPHETS

P aul says that the Church is 'built on the foundation of the apostles and prophets, with Christ Jesus himself as the chief cornerstone' (Ephesians 2:20). Unless apostles and prophets work together to help restore team ministry to its full function, we will not see the Church come to maturity and rise up to be who she should be.

Apostles

Put simply, apostles are those who are first in authority, builders, sent ones. They are fathers and mothers raising sons and daughters. I like what Dr Sam Storms says: 'apostles are first in authority but least in privilege'.[12] Apostles provide covering and empowerment to the wider body of Christ. They are master builders who help to lay the foundation of Christ in individual lives and in the Church.

Apostles have been functioning in the Church for the last 2,000 years, though they may not always have been recognised as such. Some of those we have labelled 'evangelists', 'missionaries', 'reformers' or 'revivalists' were in fact apostles. Martin Luther, John Knox, George Fox, John Wesley, Hudson Taylor, D L Moody and John G Lake are but a few examples. These, and many others, served the purpose of God in their generation and laid foundations for the generations after them. They called the Church back to the Word of God, to truth and ultimately to Jesus.

---

[12] Dr Sam Storms, from a message preached in 1995 with Mike Bickle.

As we have sought to learn more about apostles, it has become increasingly clear that their lives ought to be marked by gentleness and humility. Our friend John Alley [13] has been a real help to us in understanding some of these things more fully. Two great apostles in scripture are Moses (who demonstrates a type of apostolic grace) in the Old Testament and Jesus in the New Testament. Interestingly, with all the signs and wonders that Moses performed, he is not described as powerful, nor as one with great authority, but as a very humble man, more humble than anyone else on the face of the earth (Numbers 12:3). Similarly, the only time that Jesus describes Himself, He does so using the words, 'I am gentle and humble in heart' (Matthew 11:29). This to us has been extremely significant when thinking of apostles today and how they should live.

We are beginning to see a restoration of true servant-hearted apostles. They are fathers and mothers, not CEOs or consultants. Their roots go deep into Christ. They are spiritual men and women who are given to much prayer. From the grace that they live in, they are able to give grace and strength to others. This is far more of a spiritual impartation than one of mere human intellect or strategy. We need apostles to help restore healthy fivefold teams, and in turn the fivefold teams need to help restore the Church and bring it to maturity.

At a recent lunch meeting with a young man, whom we believe to be an emerging apostle, Steve felt the inner voice of the Lord speaking about still and premature births. This felt like a warning of the Holy Spirit that

---

[13] See resources on the Apostolic under Further Reading.

we must nurture and help the young apostles. We believe the Lord will bring forth many apostles in our day to be able to fulfil his end-time purposes. Not all apostles will be the same; some will have a town-wide influence, others will be for a region or a nation, and still others will have a grace to touch nations. One is not better than another but, 'A person can receive only what is given them from heaven' (John 3:27). We are still in a posture of learning about this whole subject and do not claim any special or unique knowledge.

Prophets

Whether it is for the days ahead or the coming decades, prophets have the ability to see from God's perspective and thus sometimes speak of the future. Prophets can bring warnings, alignment and correction to the body of Christ. They are the Lord's mouthpiece, bringing alignment and often calling people back to a life of holiness and devotion to the Lord. Their gift also helps to activate the revelatory realm for believers and churches.

In John 4, Jesus has a word of knowledge about the woman at the well. He tells her things about her life that He has no way of knowing but by revelation of the Spirit. He also speaks to her about the future and what is to come. Her response to Jesus is, 'I can see that you are a prophet.' Prophets have the ability to walk into a particular situation and see in the Spirit what needs dealing with (whether it's past wounds or sin). They can bring words of knowledge, revelation and wisdom.

Coming Together

Interestingly, as a married couple, we operate in the two gifts of the prophetic and the apostolic respectively. We often joke that, because one of us is near-sighted and the other is long-sighted in the natural, we can see much more clearly together. In the same way, our spiritual gifts complement one another; we work better together rather than in isolation.

Our personal observation is also that apostles are often thinking about building things in a sustainable, scalable way. Paul referred to himself in 1 Corinthians 3:10 as a master builder who laid the foundation of Christ. On the other hand, the prophets often help to bring clarity and detail, highlighting potential problems that need addressing. Many times, this has come as urgent warning, even a rebuke.

It is only recently that we have started learning what it means to operate in these gifts together. This has been both an exciting and a daunting journey. Over the past two years, we have begun to share the pulpit more and more and have preached and led together from a place of praying and listening to the Lord. We have not got it right every time, but we are contending for the fullness of all that God has.

Our experience has been that when we are around each other, we function better and our gifts are heightened. We sharpen each other's gifting. The prophet will give a word and the apostle knows what needs to be done next in response to that prophetic word. Together, they can help sort and lay foundations.

Apostolic Covering

The language of 'apostolic covering' is not used much today but it is something we see modelled in Scripture. We believe it needs to be rediscovered for the Church.

Spiritual covering is simply about providing grace and protection for a person or a group of people by way of having authority over them. It is from the place of relationship that the authority is given and received. It is not demanded or coerced; it is in the genuine heart connection that these things work. Spiritual covering works on many levels. Parents can provide covering for their children. Leaders can provide covering for their congregations. Apostles provide covering for churches and ministries. For parents, leaders or apostles who live righteously, there is a grace and protection that extends to cover those with whom they have true relationship. Alternatively, if a parent, leader or apostle is living with sin and hypocrisy, this will negatively affect those people over whom they hold influence. Covering is a spiritual principle, just like gravity in the natural. We must learn its value and work with it in a biblical and healthy way.

Covering is relational, not organisational. In the past, some denominations have been governed on the basis of signing certain documents and committing to particular rules or conduct. Apostolic families, on the other hand, are formed on the basis of spiritual joining. It is when we give our hearts to one another in this way that there is a greater trust, loyalty and commitment. Acknowledging and submitting to the apostolic anointing to which we are joined is a Kingdom pattern. It is in the submission one to another that we find a greater freedom and spiritual flow. The anointing of an apostle can help hold people, churches and ministries steady and strengthen them.

The Apostle Paul provided spiritual covering for many churches in the New Testament. When writing to the church in Colossae, we get a sense that he knew them, despite not having visited them (Colossians 2:5). By his persistent prayer for them and by sending letters of instruction, he was able to hold them steady. Another example is in Luke 22:31-32. Jesus tells Simon that He has been praying for him so that his faith will not fail when he is tempted. Jesus, the Chief Apostle, knows how one of His team will respond, and He can hold him in the Spirit, give him direction and know that he will come back round.

Covering is essential. We are aware of the challenges some churches have been through over the last 40-50 years as a result of the abuse of power and wrongful control of people. Yet we firmly believe we must not throw the baby out with the bathwater. Instead, our desire is to reclaim, redefine and model a gentle, humble and fatherly apostolic grace. We need to rediscover covering, its power and significance in apostolic families today and not be afraid of giving our hearts to one another despite past abuses that have occurred.

What Now?

1. Reflect on the applications from the previous chapter. Do you know where your gifting lies? How can you nurture this?

2. Seek out mentors who are further along than you in the gifting that you feel you have, to help coach you through the process of learning.

3. Reach out to us via https://allnationsmovement.org/ if you want to know more about apostolic covering and how you could be a part of an apostolic family.

Prayer

> … built on the foundation of the apostles and prophets, with Christ Jesus himself as the chief cornerstone. In him the whole building is joined together and rises to become a holy temple in the Lord.
>
> **- Ephesians 2:20-21**

Lord, I pray that You would raise up apostles and prophets on the Earth to lay the foundations needed for the coming together of the fivefold gifts as team. I pray that there would be godly mothers and fathers to help to nurture younger men and women to maturity.

Amen

_____

"Do you know that nothing you do in this life will ever matter, unless it is about loving God and loving the people He has made?"

- Francis Chan

CHAPTER 23 – GATHERING AND GOING

Throughout the New Testament, we see a pattern of gathering and going. The Early Church met together daily in their homes and in the temple (Acts 2:46), but they also went out to the towns and villages and shared the gospel (Acts 8:4).

For many churches in the West, Sunday gatherings have become the sole expression of faith in Jesus. This is one of the things we have felt the Lord putting His finger on for us during this past season. As the ability to meet together in a physical building was literally taken away because of Covid restrictions, we realised that nearly all our energy, as a church leadership team and staff, had been geared towards the Sunday services. We were neglecting His command to go. What is more, we had been fuelling a Sunday-Christianity mindset that was damaging the body of Christ. This old wineskin leads to congregations of consumers who come to church to be fed, refreshed and energised but are not generally willing to contribute to the mission of Christ themselves. The many were attending to be fed and cared for by the few. We don't blame the congregations for this, but us as leaders who have created such a system.

As Covid restrictions began to ease, and after much consideration and prayer, we made the uncomfortable decision to shift our church meeting patterns. The thinking behind this was to help our church family break out of the consumer mindset and to facilitate disciple-making. And so the phrase became, 'We gather and we go.' We have gone from meeting in the building every Sunday, as most churches currently do, to every other Sunday. This has been very painful for us and our church family, but the Lord has said to us that we cannot just speak about obedience and making disciples, but our programmes and rhythms need to empower it to happen. On the Sundays where we don't meet together in a large setting, we are encouraging people to go out and be missional in their local community. This may look like prayer walking an area, engaging in one-to-one discipleship with a non-believer or running a home church. Home church leaders are becoming the church planters in their neighbourhoods. We are taking the power away from a few people who are responsible for running a Sunday service and instead giving it back to the body of Christ.

While this may all sound exciting and fresh, the journey has not been without its challenges. Over the past two years, we have had many difficult conversations, painful misunderstandings and some who have sadly left our church family. Even for those who are still committed to the vision of the house, we have yet to see a 100% buy-in on the weeks that we are not meeting together. At the same time, we have been encouraged to hear some of the early stories of baptisms in gardens, salvation on doorsteps and people hosting weekly Bible studies for non-believing neighbours. Encouragingly, we are also witnessing a number of Christian families relocating geographically to come to be with us as the Lord has been speaking to them on their own journeys about the very same priorities.

The pattern of meeting is not the important thing. We are not advocating a new church model, nor are we suggesting that this approach will work for every church family. Rather, we are doing our best to listen to the Holy Spirit and obey His promptings every step of the way. It is a well-known phrase that 'the definition of insanity is doing the same thing over and over again and expecting different results'.[14] If the old wineskin was not producing disciples who made disciples but a congregation of consumers, we had to change it if we wanted to see different results. At least in this season, we feel that this approach has best facilitated the 'gather and go' of the gospel in our context, and we are excited to see all that the Lord will do with us and through us as we keep walking in obedience to Him. We will also do all we can to help other churches around the world to learn and grow in this.

The Importance of Gathering

Why keep meeting on a Sunday at all? Some have misunderstood our move away from the weekly Sunday gatherings as a rejection of large gatherings altogether. This is not the case. We recognise that there is great value in meeting together as a larger body of Christ. In fact, Hebrews 10:24-25 clearly tells us not to forsake the gathering of the saints. There is great power when we gather; there is encouragement when we gather; there is shared learning when we gather and there is mutual edification.

There are also different ways of gathering with other believers; different gatherings will serve different functions. Large auditorium-style events allow for powerful times of corporate worship and praise. They also provide a good space for strong apostolic teaching or preaching so that the wider family can hear about the journey of where the Lord is taking the church. Smaller gatherings in homes allow for life to be shared, prayer

---

[14] Attributed to Albert Einstein.

to be given in a more specific way and the Scriptures to be opened together. As well as embracing the smaller gatherings, we have received prophetic words about stadium gatherings coming back. We are excited by this and are believing that this will be a part of what the Lord will do in the season ahead.

Another type of gathering that we have introduced is a Saturday-night Encounter meeting at the end of each month. These evenings have involved times of extended prayer and worship. In these settings, there is space to hear from God together and we allow people to come forward and share what they feel the Lord is saying.

Although we have moved away from meeting every Sunday, we have tried to be more intentional about when we gather and to allow the different settings to serve different needs.

The Importance of Going

William Temple famously said that the Church is the only organisation that exists for its non-members. Or at least, it should be this way. Like the Dead Sea, which has an inflow without an outflow, unless we go, we can become stagnant and lifeless. Many churches that only gather with other believers seem to be constantly putting out fires. We can become self-centred and narrow in our outlook; leaders spend their energy trying to keep their congregations happy and there is very little focus on those outside the church who need the good news of Jesus.

Interestingly, the Great Commission of Jesus, in Matthew 28, starts with the little word 'Go'. While most Christians have no problem with gathering, it is this little word that we find most difficult. We must reclaim the power of the Church in its mission to go and rediscover healthy patterns for doing so.

What was difficult a hundred years ago has now been made much easier because of the speed and ease of travel. As the world has changed, so our methods of mission and disciple-making can adapt. For some, the call to go will mean travelling to other parts of the world for long periods of time or even permanently relocating. For others, there will be some travelling back and forth between countries while staying connected and accountable to a local church family. And for some, they will use creative methods through digital media to be able to connect with people. However, while not everyone will feel called to travel to other parts of the world, we are all called to be on mission wherever we are.

This is a big mindset shift for the Church in the West, and we will have to strengthen this area of our thinking because it has been weak for so long. For every believer, the call to go means sharing Jesus with our neighbours, our work colleagues, our family and our friends. These are the people that God has placed around us, and this is our primary mission field. We must have a readiness to share and a posture of prayerful listening for where the Lord is opening doors.

What Now?

We cannot overstate the importance of the prayer journey. In the place of prayer, we begin to change as individuals and we start to see the world differently. The first reaction ought not to be to change the programme. The first reaction is to take what you are reading and hearing, to explore the Scriptures and then to commit to pray.

For those in church leadership:

1. If your leadership team or eldership team haven't been reading this book with you, invite them to join you in reading it. Together, you can then go on a journey of prayerfully discerning what God is saying in your context.

2. Both individually and as a team, read through New Testament passages like the Great Commission (in Matthew 28) and the stories of the Early Church in Acts. Wrestle with the following questions:

   - Is there a gap between what we read and what we are doing today?

   - How did we get to where we are today?

   - Are we producing disciples? If not, why not?

3. Before making major changes, it can be helpful to explore these topics further. One helpful resource is our All Nations Storehouse platform. This contains free eCourses, articles and podcasts on the subject of church-planting, discipleship and the coming revival.[15]

---

[15] See resources on disciple-making under Further Reading.

For those not in church leadership:

1. Start with prayer. Ask the Lord to help you to see your neighbours, friends, family and colleagues as He does.

2. Commit to prayer walking your local area once or twice a week. This will not only shift the spiritual atmosphere of your neighbourhood but will also change your own perspective and allow you to see things differently. On the All Nations Movement app, you can find some useful tools about how to do this.[16]

3. You may want to give this book to your church leader so that they can consider whether to go on the journey themselves.

Prayer

> He told them, 'The harvest is plentiful, but the workers are few. Ask the Lord of the harvest, therefore, to send out workers into his harvest field. Go! I am sending you out like lambs among wolves.'
> **- Luke 10:2-3**

Thank You, Lord, that You are reforming Your Church and changing its priorities. I pray that You would empower the Church not only to gather, but also to go out and make disciples. Anoint me for this work, I pray. Amen

---

[16] Search 'All Nations Movement app' on Google Play store or Apple App store.

"Behold, I will send you Elijah the prophet before the great and awesome day of the Lord comes. And he will turn the hearts of fathers to their children and the hearts of children to their fathers..."

- Malachi 4:5-6a

CHAPTER 24 -

APOSTOLIC CENTRES EMERGING

P eter describes followers of Christ as 'living stones' being built into a spiritual house (1 Peter 2:5). If the new wineskin is people, then the building blocks for the new are living stones. Our friend Akhtar Shah has often drawn the comparison between living stones with which the Lord is building His Church and the bricks used in the story of the Tower of Babel. In Genesis 11:3, it says that the people baked bricks instead of using stone. While the people in this story had ingenuity to attempt to get to heaven, every brick was the same and produced in a factory line, and we know they were ultimately unsuccessful. Stones, in contrast, are all slightly different shapes and sizes. It takes more effort to figure out how they fit together but it leads to greater strength and beauty in a structure. If we try to force people and churches into standard brick moulds, we will stunt growth. Rather, we must embrace the unique gifting and calling of every believer, church and wider family.

This is why, for the majority of this book, we have tried to avoid describing models and practical structures. We firmly believe that the Lord does not want a cookie-cutter approach in His people. This has been a major downfall of the last season, which is marked by fascination with church growth, structures and models. No two leaders are the same, and therefore no two churches will look the same.

Nevertheless, we felt it was important to include a chapter that talks about some of what we feel is unfolding on the Earth in terms of practical structures, principles and what this looks like in our own context. It is important to include a disclaimer at this stage and to say that this is still an unfolding picture. We don't have all aspects of it up and functioning yet. There are some elements that are currently working really well and other parts yet to emerge and pick up momentum. If you want to see how it develops over the coming season, we encourage you to follow the All Nations Movement.[17]

We believe that the Lord is raising up Apostolic Centres on the Earth. There were at least three key Apostolic Centres in the New Testament: Jerusalem, Antioch and Ephesus. As we read the New Testament, we see that these were hubs of tremendous spiritual activity. They were strongholds for the Kingdom of God, training and sending people (Acts 13:1-3). They helped to oversee churches and ministries. They were places of the presence of God, of worship and of fasting. They were also places that people were drawn to and sent from.

What Is an Apostolic Centre?

Every Apostolic Centre will be unique because of the creativity of the Holy Spirit, and the particular calling of the people and the place. Yet they will all have defining principles. There are perhaps three defining principles that we currently see, although these are not exclusive or exhaustive.

First, Apostolic Centres have apostolic foundations; they are formed around the anointing of an apostle. It is this anointing that makes it

---

[17] See resources on disciple-making under Further Reading.

different from other models of church that we have seen dominate recent history. Most churches are centred on a pastoral anointing or grace. There is usually one man or woman, with a pastoral gift, who cares for the people, takes responsibility for marrying and burying and visits members of the congregation in their homes. This model often defaults to a focus on maintenance. Centres that build around the apostolic anointing will have much more of a missional focus and take on a spirit of advance. While there is a place for pastoral churches, we believe they need to come into connection with emerging Apostolic Centres to be holistic, healthy and well rounded.

Second, an Apostolic Centre will consist of an apostolic people. We believe that this refers to relational joining in the Spirit and unity. There is a genuine loving and giving of heart. We see this in the Early Church who sacrificially gave of their finances, property and lives for one another. It is the apostolic grace that forms the apostolic people. We have lived in a generation where there has been a strong emphasis on leadership but not necessarily on relationship. Apostolic Centres will see spiritual fathers and mothers emerging and raising up true sons and daughters (Malachi 4:6). The next move of God will be about releasing the people of God into the fullness of who they are.

Third, Apostolic Centres will be committed to an apostolic mission or mandate. They will be obedient to the Great Commission of Jesus to make disciples of all nations and will be sending centres. We see in Acts 13 that Paul and Barnabas were sent off on the instruction of the Holy Spirit. Not only will people be sent out to the nations, but these centres will also be integrated into the communities in which they are based and will take on an element of social action. Those who are sent will remain a part of the apostolic family, who will support them in prayer, relationship, people and finances.

'Teams of teams' is a phrase that has kept coming back to us over this past season. In contrast to the more traditional pyramid model, where one person is at the top, leading everyone else, we believe God is bringing about teams. It feels as though there are going to be circles within circles that will overlap, and strong relationships are essential. Over the last few years, we have seen new teams begin to emerge in the All Nations Apostolic Movement. Whether it is a senior team bringing oversight to the whole thing, a team helping with the UK vision, a team emerging in the US or a team emerging for youth and young adults, God has been raising groups of people who all help to share the load. Though in the past, there have been some men and women who have been instrumental in God's hand, we believe that, in these last days, He is raising a nameless, faceless army on the Earth.

What Has it Looked Like Practically?

Very early on, as we started to think about what an Apostolic Centre might look like, we knew that disciple-making would be a key building block. Disciples are the starting point. Every individual disciple must be committed to making disciples. At this initial level, there may be two or three people who are relationally accountable to one another and are committed to growing in their Christlikeness.

At the next level, these groups of disciples will form churches. We call these 'home churches' or 'missional communities'. These churches may meet in homes, parks, community centres, prisons or university buildings, to name a few places. But while they will all be slightly different,[18] they will all carry the hallmarks of the Early Church in Acts 2:42-47. They will be 'devoted … to the apostles' teaching and to fellowship, to the breaking of bread and to prayer'. They will see signs and wonders, have everything in common, sell property and possessions to give to those in need, meet regularly, praise God and enjoy the favour of all the people. They will be missional in their outlook. Genuine community will be formed in these places.

At the next level, these churches will come together with other churches in a region or neighbourhood to form a cluster. A cluster may be made up of four to five churches. They will together take a strong responsibility for a given area. We have grown, and will continue to grow, teams of home church overseers who take responsibility for looking after these clusters.

At the level above this, we can also see gatherings where clusters all meet together periodically, in a region or a town. These times will include space to hear the apostles' teaching and to share testimony about what God is doing.

---

[18] Helpful short video to understand 'Church' - 4Fields. (nd). *Church Circle* (Acts 2:36-47) [Video]. YouTube. https://youtu.be/ftf_2Gq_-Co (Accessed 27 June 2022).

Small groups of disciples may be meeting every two or three days. Churches may be meeting weekly. Clusters may be meeting monthly. The regional gathering may happen bi-monthly. This is what we are working towards.

Practical Resources

Along our journey, we have picked up some helpful practical tools from different resources. Many of these have come from the Disciple Making Movement (DMM) teaching. Discovery Bible Studies (DBS)[19] are great ways for small groups of disciples or churches to be able to explore the Bible together and with non-believers. We do not want to go into detail about these things in this book, but would encourage you to read Chris Galanos' book, *From Megachurch to Multiplication*.[20]

Another key element is generational mapping. This is a way of seeing how churches are multiplying and whether they are carrying Acts 2 traits as they multiply.[21]

---

[19] Zúme Training gives a good explanation of what we mean by DMM and DBS. See resources on disciple-making under Further Reading.

[20] Chris Galanos, *From Megachurch to Multiplication: A Church's Journey Toward Movement* (Lubbock, Tx: Experience Life, 2018).

[21] Disciple Tools is a helpful software tool for tracking disciples and groups. See resources on disciple-making under Further Reading.

What Now?

1. If you feel that you have an apostolic gifting and desire to set up an Apostolic Centre, we would strongly encourage you not to do it on your own. Walking relationally with other apostles is really helpful. What we see happening across the world is Apostolic Centres rising and connecting to other Apostolic Centres. In this way, the Lord will form a huge net across regions, nations and even the world.

2. Try to avoid defining too quickly what you are becoming. The aim is not to become experts. We want to live from a place of listening to the Holy Spirit and only forming as He reveals things to us. The journey is just as important as the destination.

Prayer

And I tell you that you are Peter, and on this rock I will build my church, and the gates of Hades will not overcome it.
- Matthew 16:18

Father, thank You for what You are doing on the Earth in our days. Thank You that we get to be part of a great storyline that is unfolding. Would You help me to find the part I am to play and where I belong?
Amen

Part VI: Pruning

In this section, we have grouped together some of the revelations that relate to a dying and a cutting away of certain things. Like the process of pruning a plant, these lessons have been uncomfortable and have, at times, made us feel vulnerable and bare. Yet the Father is both good and a skilled gardener; He knows what He is doing, which will be for our good and His glory. We believe that these lessons will eventually lead to greater fruitfulness in our lives, and we pray that you are willing to embrace them too.

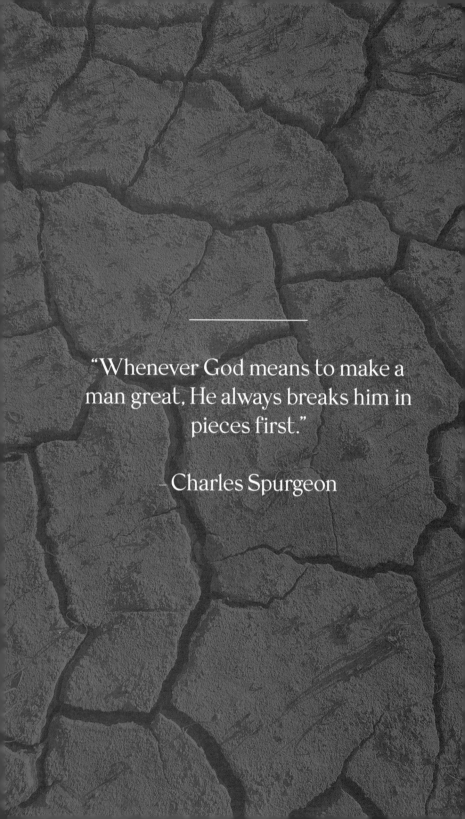

———————

"Whenever God means to make a
man great, He always breaks him in
pieces first."

– Charles Spurgeon

CHAPTER 25 - CUTTING TO CURE

The Lord speaks in numerous ways to His people, and one of those ways is through family and the circumstances we go through. Our daughter Sophia has walked through some challenging health issues and, with her permission, we wanted to share briefly some of the parallels we felt with her journey and the journey of the Church.

Sophia first started being unwell a couple of years ago. After numerous visits to the doctor, and even seeing different doctors, she had been prescribed various medicines but no firm diagnosis of what was wrong. The medication she took did not work; if anything, it seemed to be making things worse. It wasn't until she had a private consultation with a doctor that she was diagnosed with an extremely rare disease. Following this, a tumour was found on her pituitary gland at the base of her brain.

Sophia was given two options. She could live with the tumour and keep taking hormone medication to counter its effects, but this would lead to a diminished life and a much higher risk of mortality (four times higher than the average person). Or she could have the tumour removed by surgery. This was an extremely risky process; it would be intrusive and painful and interrupt all of her plans for a season. There would be a long recovery time but, ultimately, if it worked, it would lead to a higher quality of life and greatly reduce the risk of mortality.

She decided to go ahead with surgery and the tumour was successfully removed in January 2022. The surgery was very traumatic for her, and in some ways, for us as a whole family watching her go through such a trial. There were moments in her recovery when she was in such pain and disorientation that she questioned whether she should have gone through with the surgery. Though we are still believing God for complete breakthrough, most of her symptoms have slowly been going away and she is in the process of being restored to full health. We are deeply grateful.

For too long, the Church has been unhealthy and has lived with negative symptoms. Some of these symptoms fall within the umbrella of 'worldliness'. We hope you don't hear us incorrectly as we write this chapter. We love and believe in the Church and will always be a strong part of the Church. Also, we recognise that much of what we have discerned as negative or unhelpful has also been in our own lives and ministry. Our aim is not to point a finger and bring accusation but to recognise the problems and, by God's grace, to move towards better health.

We are reminded of the tale of The Emperor's New Clothes. Though the Emperor was naked, he had been deceived to believe he was fully clothed in the latest and most fashionable wardrobe. With much pomp and ceremony, he celebrated his new clothes through a public fashion show. Though he was completely naked, the deception was so prevalent that everybody still applauded him. That was until a child spoke out that the Emperor had no clothes on.

In some ways, because the Church has lived with unhealthy symptoms for so long, we've been like the people in the story who collectively went along with the narrative they were being told. If we were to read the

Gospels and the book of Acts for the very first time, with no conscious awareness of the last 2,000 years of Church history, we would perhaps realise how starkly different the Church is today compared to the Early Church.

One of the negative symptoms in the Church has been the mixture that has been allowed in. Though we profess to be followers of Christ, the lifestyles of many, our value systems and our treatment of each other doesn't seem to be particularly different from the world that surrounds us. The mixture in our lives has diminished our fruitfulness to the degree that we have yet to see radical, lasting transformation in our communities. Father God is so wonderfully gracious that, even in this state, the Church has been allowed to see a measure of fruit and to bring God's light into our communities.

Some churches are faithful in preaching the gospel and seeing people making commitments to follow Christ. We would be among the first to acknowledge the genuine sincerity and faithfulness of many Christians. Yet, at the same time, it doesn't take away from the fact that we have settled far below the Lord's original design and intent.

The believers in the New Testament caused massive transformation in towns and regions, and the Lord desires for this to happen today (see Acts 8:4-8; 19:18-20). Many in the Church have prayed 'the sinner's prayer', but this isn't the same as being deeply in love with Jesus and committed to radical, obedient discipleship. Paul Cain, whose own life was controversial, often used the phrase when preaching, 'To a people without mixture, the Lord will give His Spirit without measure.'[22]

Another symptom that the Church has been displaying is its spiritual weakness. We have had a form of godliness but have been lacking true spiritual power (2 Timothy 3:5). Generally speaking, we have lacked power to see the miraculous, though we are encouraged by what is happening and there are heartening stories around the world of miracles and healings. Yet we recognise that when we read about the life of Jesus and the disciples and then look at our lives today, there is a discrepancy for most believers in the Western Church. Power is not only for miracles, signs and wonders, but also to live godly lives. This is shown as we forgive those who hurt or mistreat us and love freely even when it is difficult. Perhaps most importantly, spiritual strength is also needed to cultivate healthy, enduring marriages and raise children in a godly way. We recognise that this may be painful for some to read, and we would reiterate that we include ourselves as part of the unhealthy Church, and desire that the Lord's full power would break in and through us. As we write this today, we pause and pray for your marriage, family, children and health. May the Lord answer the deepest cry of your heart in bringing the needed breakthrough.

Furthermore, there has been a toxic consumer culture that has crept into the Church. People attend a service once a week, often focused on having their needs met – to feel better about themselves, enjoy 'the worship

---

[22] Eternal Classics (2020 Sep 17) *Paul Cain interviewed by Mike Bickle (1990) His Life, Supernatural Miracles, Healings & Revelation P1'* [Video] YouTube, https://youtu.be/yYfDkIhrw5I (accessed 8 July 2022).

experience' and meet a few friends. Many have strong opinions about what the worship style should be and who their favourite worship leader is. The length of service, preaching and kind of children's work all play a part in people moving around to different churches to find the place and the people who will best meet their needs and preferences. This is not a healthy picture. It is not the Church that the Lord intended and seems to be in opposition to the call of Jesus:

> Anyone who loves their father or mother more than me is not worthy of me; anyone who loves their son or daughter more than me is not worthy of me. Whoever does not take up their cross and follow me is not worthy of me. Whoever finds their life will lose it, and whoever loses their life for my sake will find it.
> - **Matthew 10:37-39**

We have often treated these symptoms as isolated issues and prescribed surface-level treatments. As church leaders, we may have tried to medicate these problems by exercising more control. As in a dysfunctional family, we take away the freedom of the children to think and act for themselves and instead try to manage and control everything ourselves in our attempts to avoid major issues.

Others may have tried to medicate through human leadership styles, relying on personality and charisma to draw people to themselves and their buildings. Strong leadership is not always healthy leadership. A person can be skilled in oratory and able to evoke emotion within a congregation, but this is not the same as being anointed. Sadly, many can no longer tell the difference between well-honed natural gifts that seek to subtly control and true spiritual power. It is only the anointing that can reach into a person's heart, break the power of the enemy and bring about true repentance.

We believe in counselling and godly pastoral care that can be very helpful for individuals and couples. But equally, some issues don't need months or years of counselling but rather an encounter with God's power to bring freedom and correct thinking. His power leads to freedom from addictions, relational healing and restoration, even restoration of a person's mind. We are not advocating one above the other but we have noted that, in our experience of 20-plus years, there has been a stronger leaning towards counselling than spiritually discerning and then praying.

Pride is perhaps the root issue in all of this. We have already looked at the importance of humility in Chapter 17, 'Go Low', so we won't focus too much on it here. The offshoots of pride are self-sufficiency, self-preservation and self-promotion. These are toxic to building true church and lead to many of the issues we have listed above. Jesus is the head of the body, His Church (Colossians 1:18). Unless He builds the Church, those who build it labour in vain (Psalm 127:1). The Lord Jesus is coming back for a takeover and He will remove all human-made ideas and 'self' from His bride.

So what are we to do? Surface-level treatments, like plasters, can only do so much. Like Sophia's decision to have surgery, it is only when we are willing to undergo a more painful process, allowing God to remove the toxic root of the issue, that the Church will regain its health. Over the last two years, we have felt as though we have been on an operating table. There have been times when we have wanted to jump off because it was too painful. Even after being on the journey for more than two years, it feels like there are still areas of our lives and ministry that the Lord is working on. We are learning not to rush His process but are seeking to come to a place of trusting that He is the master surgeon who loves us and knows what is best. Our best response is to patiently submit to His work.

At a recent appointment for Sophia, we told the nurse that Sophia was still feeling unusually tired. The nurse explained that they were giving her just enough medication to get by in the hope that, by depriving her of the full amount of hormones needed, the rest of her body would wake up and function as it should do to produce what was needed. They were being cruel to be kind. God, in His kindness, may withhold things from us in order that we are reactivated to live and function as He originally designed us.

We looked at the Lord's rebuke to the Laodicean church in Revelation 3 in an earlier chapter. Though they were wealthy and had a high opinion of themselves, in the eyes of Jesus there were some things that were really wrong. He called them, 'wretched, pitiful, poor, blind and naked' (verse 17). Though this seems like a harsh way for Jesus to speak, He says in verse 19 that He rebukes and disciplines those He loves. It is because the Lord loves us and sees our potential that He will be honest as to our unhealthy condition. Like with the Laodicean church, He counsels us to come to Him so that we may be restored to full health.

Yet you, LORD, are our Father.

We are the clay, you are the potter;

we are all the work of your hand.

- **Isaiah 64:8**

The picture of being on the potter's wheel and allowing Him to shape, and sometimes to squash the clay and rebuild, is another really helpful analogy. We must surrender to our loving Father as He makes us and moulds us into the healthy Church that we were created to be.

What Now?

1. Take some time to consider prayerfully whether any of these negative symptoms have been present in your own life. Ask the Lord to reveal to you where you may have been treating these as isolated and surface level rather than getting to the root of the issue.

2. If you are in church leadership or part of a team, why not read through this chapter together? Invite the Holy Spirit to reveal to you any areas that you have tried to medicate yourselves, whether that be through human management, leadership or other strategies. Surrender these things to the Lord and ask Him to begin the operation process.

Prayer

Out of the depths I cry to you, LORD;

Lord, hear my voice.

Let your ears be attentive to my cry for mercy.

If you, LORD, kept a record of sins,

Lord, who could stand?

But with you there is forgiveness,

so that we can, with reverence, serve you.

- Psalm 130:1-4

Amen

"The moral project for a Christian is to die to the old self and rise to new life in Christ... Dying and rising - the rhythm of a life of discipleship - names the process by which we grow accustomed to a life more and more like Christ."

- Rebecca Konyndyk DeYoung

CHAPTER 26 - LET IT FALL AND DIE

Very truly I tell you, unless a kernel of wheat falls to the ground
and dies, it remains only a single seed. But if it dies, it produces
many seeds.

- John 12:24

With the promise of revival and an unprecedented harvest of souls,
it is easy to get excited about the new life that is coming into
the Kingdom. What is clear from this verse in John 12 is that death is
needed if new life is to come forth. Without a death, there can be no
resurrection. The Kingdom of God to which we belong is unlike the
world in which we live. It is a backwards kingdom where the last are first,
the poor are rich and death means life. We have realised afresh in this
season that we must fight popular culture that promotes self-protection
and self-preservation. As long as we try to hold on to our life, we will lose
it (Matthew 16:25). It is only in the dying that we will see true life
springing forth – not only in ourselves but also in the fruit of an
end-time harvest.

One of the areas that we have had to die to in this past season is
our reputation. There have been multiple conversations we have had with
different people and multiple misunderstandings. We have had people
leave our church family and we have had people saying hurtful things.
While there has been a temptation to justify our decisions and defend
our actions, we have felt the restraint of the Holy Spirit and a sense that
we need to let go.

There will be different challenges for all of us as we step out in obedience to Christ. There are believers today all around the world who are literally laying down their lives for the gospel. While this is not necessarily the call of every believer, we all have to deny ourselves and take up our cross if we are to follow Jesus (Matthew 16:24). It may be dying to the desire for financial security, to our comforts or to the fear of other people.

In the current days in which we live, political correctness seems to have gone crazy. There is a real fear of what people might say, and even of the legal consequences we may face for certain statements. When we replace our fears with the fear of God, we will be able to overcome the challenges of our culture. Our friend Lawrence Neisent gives the example of a man on a bridge over a lake being encouraged by his friends to join them in the water below, but he is afraid to jump and so he hesitates. When a high-speed train comes to cross the bridge and he realises there is no room to remain on the bridge, the lesser fear submits to the greater fear and he jumps. This is how the fear of the Lord works in our lives: it will cause all lesser fears to submit and be removed in the presence of the Lord.

We can take encouragement from the men and women in the Bible who let things die so they could follow the Lord's calling. When Elisha was called to follow Elijah, he burnt the twelve oxen on his ploughing equipment (1 Kings 19:21). This had been his source of income and represented all he had known before. He was willing to sacrifice financial security to follow the Lord's call. When Esther was chosen as Queen, she was willing to approach the King unsummoned, even though this act was punishable by death, to save her people (Esther 4:1; 5:1-2).

She risked losing her life to obey the Lord's call. When Joseph received the dreams of leadership (Genesis 37–41), he was willing to endure slavery and prison before seeing them come to pass. He sacrificed his reputation and his rights as a free man to follow the Lord. Before David took his place on the throne of Israel, he spent years running in the wilderness, and in doing so, he died to his reputation. Jesus Himself left the comfort of heaven, took on human form with all its limitations, suffered the misunderstandings of humanity and ultimately hung on the cross. These people embraced the dying process because they knew there would be great reward on the other end of their obedience. It is in the dying that new life comes and doors are opened.

How Do We Die to Self?

There are moments in our lives when big and dramatic circumstances can lead to significant change, but dying to self is not a one-time act. Rather, there are hundreds of smaller decisions to die to self that we must make each and every day. This may look like asking for forgiveness when we realise we have been harsh or critical with our words. It may mean apologising to our spouse or children for allowing anger to take over. It may mean staying silent though no one credits us for the work that we have done. Small decisions to humble ourselves help to form the character of Christ in us. Though we make ourselves weak when we do this, the Lord promises that His grace will be sufficient. It is in our weakness that His power is made perfect (2 Corinthians 12:9). The Apostle Paul is a shining example of such a life because he knew that these 'light and momentary troubles' were achieving an eternal weight in glory (2 Corinthians 4:17).

Another way we can die to self is by embracing trials without complaint. Isaiah prophesied about Jesus that, like 'a sheep before its shearers is silent', He would not open his mouth when suffering (Isaiah 53:7). We know that this is true. Jesus did not defend Himself when He stood trial before Pilate. Though He had every reason to, though the accusations of the people were false and His reputation and life were about to be taken, Jesus did not speak in His own defence. Instead, He willingly submitted to the Father's plan.

The same is true for us. We are not only to endure trials but also to worship our way through them (Psalm 8:1-2). Smith Wigglesworth said that 'every trial is a lift, every burden a place of exchanging strength'.[23] Whether it's the loss of a job, a negative medical diagnosis, relational disappointment or an overwhelming bill, when we look to the Lord in these moments, He can use the situations for our good and for His glory (Romans 8:28). We have been learning in the last two years how to take painful circumstances to the Lord in the place of prayer – sometimes to ask for the things to change, other times for grace to endure and all the time for wisdom to see things from His perspective. If we are to step into all that the Lord has for us and partner with Him in what He is doing on the Earth, we must die to self. There is a painful process of releasing our ideas, letting go of our rights and dying to our reputation. Like a seed falling into the ground, we must let these things fall and die. The Lord will not share His glory with another. 'He must become greater; I must become less' (John 3:30).

---

[23] Smith Wigglesworth, in his sermon *The Ministry of the Flaming Sword*.

What Now?

1. Reflect on whether there are areas of your life that need to die. Are there things that you struggle to let go of? Make a note of these in your journal and commit to surrendering them to the Lord in the place of prayer.

2. Ask the Holy Spirit to open your eyes and to give you an eternal perspective so that the things of this world will lose their hold. Surrender your life to Jesus again.

Prayer

I have been crucified with Christ and I no longer live, but Christ lives in me. The life I now live in the body, I live by faith in the Son of God, who loved me and gave himself for me.
- **Galatians 2:20**

Lord, thank You for the example of Jesus. Thank You for His life, death and resurrection. Give me courage to deny myself, take up my cross and follow You. I am crucified with You and no longer live, but I desire for You to live in me. Thank You that You are the resurrection and the life.
Amen

"There comes a time when we must stop mourning for the old, embrace the new and advance."

– Steve Uppal

CHAPTER 27 - MOURNING TO MOVEMENT

T he last two years of significant changes to our church patterns and rhythms have caused us to ask questions and to reflect on the best way forward, and sometimes even to question ourselves. Along the way, we have faced misunderstandings as well as challenging and emotional conversations. We have come up against many questions that we don't always have the answers to. The journey has been really painful, and we have often mourned over relationships, the struggle and the way things were before.

Following the death of something, mourning is a normal process, but there comes a point where we must move on. There have been many restless nights where one or both of us have gone downstairs, unable to sleep, and taken our anxiety or pain to the Lord. A few months ago I (Steve), unable to sleep at 2am, went downstairs and sat at the dining room table feeling a sense of overwhelming grief, when suddenly the Lord spoke very clearly from 1 Samuel 16: 'How long will you mourn over that which I have rejected?'

Without going into the full details of that significant experience, let us share the wisdom we gained through it. We felt the Lord highlight two Old Testament stories that relate to the importance of going from *mourning to movement*.

The first story can be found in 1 Samuel 15 and 16. The Lord rejects King Saul because of his disobedience to the Lord's instructions. Saul's kingship began with the Spirit of God coming on him powerfully and he prophesied with the prophets (1 Samuel 10:10). We also read in 1 Samuel 11 that the Spirit of the Lord came on him, and in great power he led the people into battle and won a mighty victory, bringing deliverance for Israel. But Saul became presumptuous and proud, and he stopped obeying the Lord. He was called, chosen and served well for a time, but then he became more concerned with his position and success rather than serving the Lord's purposes. He became self-reliant and no longer feared the Lord. Samuel found it difficult to let go of Saul, and it says in 1 Samuel 15:35 that he mourned for him. It is in this context that the Lord asks Samuel how long he will mourn over that which the Lord has rejected.

The second story can be found in Joshua 1. The Lord reminds Joshua that Moses is dead and that he must now cross over into the Promised Land. Joshua was well aware that Moses had died. By reminding him of this fact, the Lord was emphasising that one season was over and a new one was beginning. Perhaps Joshua, like Samuel, was mourning what had been. Moses was the great deliverer of the people. He performed some of the most outstanding miracles we read about in the Bible; he talked to God face to face and served the Lord well, but his season was over. For 40 years, the people of Israel had wandered around the desert living a nomadic lifestyle. Now they were about to start taking land and territory and setting up permanent homes. Joshua had to take the people from an old way of behaving into a new way of thinking. He could only do this if he was willing to let go of the old.

In both of these stories, one season had ended and another was awaiting. Unless the people were willing to let go of what had been, they would have been unable to enter the new, fresh and better things that lay ahead. Whether it is letting go of things that the Lord is displeased with or letting go of good things that have simply served their purpose, we must move from a place of mourning if we are to step into all that God has for us. The Lord's instruction to Samuel was to get up and anoint David. If we are to overcome mourning, we have to change our posture to see and move with the new.

Both of these stories fit into the pruning process that we read about in John 15.

> I am the true vine, and my Father is the gardener. He cuts off every branch in me that bears no fruit, while every branch that does bear fruit he prunes so that it will be even more fruitful.
> **- John 15:1-2**

There are two cuttings mentioned in this passage. First, the Lord cuts off the things that are dead and are no longer producing fruit. Second, the Lord cuts back the branches that are bearing fruit but could be more fruitful. As we have been on a process of letting things die, we have been learning that some things we were doing were human-made and didn't bear fruit. Like with Saul, the Lord is cutting away self-reliance and autonomy from His people. There were also some things, like the life of Moses, that we had been doing that had been good in their season, but these also needed to be cut back so that we could become even more fruitful. In both cases, there is a temptation to allow the grieving to become debilitating. There will rightly be some opportunity to mourn and recognise the pain of the journey, but it must not immobilise us from forward movement, nor from what the Lord is asking.

Fight the Familiar

When moving into something new, there are times when our hearts long for the comfort of that with which we are familiar. This is true in the natural and it is also true in the spiritual. We are creatures of habit and routines, and we develop patterns of comfort in the way that we live. When these comforts are disrupted, it leads to us feeling vulnerable and awkward. The natural response is to go back to the comfortable. We must resist this urge and fight the comfort of the familiar. Whether it be the way we have done ministry or run our programmes, we must be willing to pioneer a new path. We will be able to do this if we are rooted firmly in an active, living relationship with the Lord and thereby our hearts are full of conviction for what He has said.

During the first few months of the pandemic in 2020, many people were asking the question, 'What is God saying and doing?' Some even began to embrace the journey of following the Holy Spirit into the new. As time went on, however, and as restrictions lifted, many defaulted to the comfort of the familiar and resorted to what they knew. We must trust that, like in the Old Testament stories, the promise is better than anything we may leave behind. King David became the greatest king for the people of Israel, and the Promised Land was exceedingly better than the wilderness. We must stop mourning and embrace moving forward.

What Now?

1. Read through Joshua 1 and 1 Samuel 16.

2. Be honest with yourself as to whether there are things from a past season that you are grieving over or are reluctant to leave behind. Ask the Lord for help to not grieve any more.

3. Just as Samuel was instructed to get up and anoint David, how can you change your posture to accept the new? Perhaps there are physical things you need to let go of. Perhaps you need to stop rehearsing the past in your mind. Meditate on the new more than you reminisce about the old.

Prayer

> Forget the former things;
> do not dwell on the past.
> See, I am doing a new thing!
> Now it springs up;
> do you not perceive it?
> I am making a way in the wilderness
> and streams in the wasteland.
> **- Isaiah 43:18-19**

Lord, would You help us to let go of that which has died and that which no longer bears fruit? We want to forget the former things and not dwell on the past. Help us to fight the comforts of the familiar.
Amen

"God has a plan for His Church upon earth. But alas! We too often make our plan, and we think that we know what ought to be done. We ask God first to bless our feeble efforts, instead of absolutely refusing to go unless God go before us."

- Andrew Murray

CHAPTER 28 - PULL OF THE PRAGMATIC

Another phrase that we felt kept coming back to us was, 'Resist the pull of the pragmatic.' To be pragmatic in our response is to be sensible, realistic and practical as opposed to basing our response on principles, or in our case as Christians on what God says. For every decision that needs to be made, there will always be a pragmatic response that could be given. We have had to fight the temptation to go along with external pressures and voices that seem to make a lot of natural sense. The Lord is not leading His people to follow human thinking but to have eyes to see what He is saying and doing. Faith is having confidence in what we do not yet see (Hebrews 11:1).

Jesus Himself faced the temptation to follow pragmatic voices. In Matthew 26, when the lady with an alabaster jar pours out the expensive nard at his feet, Jesus' disciples make a seemingly sensible suggestion – that the money could have been better used if given away to charity. Jesus, however, doesn't agree with them. He says that the act of worship was what was needed in that moment. He sees the bigger picture and does not look merely through human eyes and reasoning. Similarly, in Mark 6, Jesus' disciples make a pragmatic suggestion to send the crowds of people away to get food. It is late, the people are in a remote place and, in the natural, it seems like a logical and reasonable thing to do. Yet Jesus' response does not sound practical or realistic. Jesus replies, 'You give them something to eat' (Mark 6:37).

We must be ever so careful which voices we listen to. Many objections that we have faced during this time of transition have seemed like wisdom but have in fact been the voice of fear. In Mark 8:33, Jesus calls one of His own disciples 'Satan' because he does not have in mind the concerns of God but 'merely human concerns'. This is a startling response by Jesus, and it can seem like an overreaction. We know that Jesus sees more clearly than we do and calls Himself the Truth (John 14:6). If Jesus labels 'merely human concerns' as demonic, then we ought to view them this seriously too. No matter how subtle, making decisions based on human 'wisdom' will eventually lead people and ministries away from the Lord.

If we were to be honest, how many of our decisions, whether in leadership meetings or coming from church discussions, are based on what is sensible, realistic and pragmatic? What would Jesus say to the Church today if He were to hear some of the rationale for our decision-making? Do we have in mind the concerns of God or merely human concerns?

The Church has lived in the pragmatic realm for so long that anything else seems foreign and strange. The shift from human thinking towards being filled with God's concerns is seismic. It demands that individuals, leaders and teams relearn how to handle team meetings and decision-making. This takes time, and we must be extremely intentional. It is not that we are to ignore the practical decisions that need to be made. Rather, they must not lead or govern more than the leading of the Holy Spirit. This way of operating may seem, to the casual observer, childlike and perhaps lacking excellence. Yet Jesus Himself taught us that unless we become like little children, we cannot enter the kingdom of God (Matthew 18:3).

Settling for Good Enough

As we travel into the new that God has for us, there will be a temptation to settle along the way. In Genesis 11 we read the story of Abraham's father, Terah, and his family. The whole family set out to go to Canaan, but when they got to Haran they settled there. The Bible tells us that eventually Terah died in Haran.

Instead of travelling to the Promised Land that God had revealed to them, they settled in a place that was 'good enough'. Perhaps Terah settled because it seemed like the sensible thing to do. Maybe it was a pragmatic response: why make the children travel further? Isn't there enough food here? The land here is good enough. Why travel and risk disappointment or injury along the way? Sadly, many of God's people settle in the place of 'good enough' instead of facing the risks that come with travelling to God's best. We must learn to fight both the external and internal pragmatic voices and contend for the fullness of what the Lord has.

Living from Rest

As we have transitioned from the old to the new, we have found that it is easy to become anxious and fearful. Not only is this discouraging to us, but we have also realised it affects those around us too. Anxiety is not a good place to lead from. It causes instability in families, teams and congregations. Anxiety can come because of pragmatic concerns. Rather than allow anxiety to rule our emotions, we must learn how to cast our cares on the Lord. We must go to the place of prayer and the place of promise. We can be honest with God about how we are feeling and remind Him of what He has promised us in Scripture or through others. When we do this, the peace of God fills our hearts. We must learn to make prayer our first response and not allow the spirit of anxiety to operate in us.

Jesus Himself is our sabbath rest, and we are told to make every effort to enter that rest (Hebrews 4:11). This is not only available for all believers, but essential, if we are to be the change agents He has called us to be. In an increasingly anxious world, those who live in sabbath rest will bring hope and life to all around them.

What Now?

It will be impossible to be led by the Spirit in corporate settings if we are not living that way in the private place.

1. Ask the Holy Spirit to lead you in daily decisions that you make.

2. If you are in church leadership or are responsible for leading a team, sit down together and prayerfully evaluate the way you make decisions. Have you been making them purely pragmatically? Ask the Lord to help you make your decisions from faith and not pragmatism.

3. If you have found that you have a tendency to become anxious, how can you cultivate a first response of prayer?

Prayer

Jesus turned and said to Peter. 'Get behind me, Satan! You are a
stumbling-block to me; you do not have in mind the concerns of
God, but merely human concerns.'
- Matthew 16:23

*Lord, would You renew our minds, that we would live with the concerns of
God and not merely human concerns? We want to live lives led by the Spirit
and not lives led by pragmatism.*
Amen

"Our heavenly Father never takes anything from His children unless He means to give them something better."

– George Muller

CHAPTER 29 -

DISMANTLE AND DECLUTTER

A nother phrase that we felt the Lord give to us is that we are to 'prayerfully and carefully dismantle and declutter'.

Dismantle

To dismantle something is to carefully take it apart in such a way that all its pieces remain useable. This was a really helpful word for us to refer to. There was a temptation, as we felt the invitation into the new, to completely discard the old. As we have already said regarding wineskins, the old does not have to be destroyed but can be made fresh again.

Whether it is the dismantling of programmes, structures or teams, we felt the need to go carefully because there were people connected to these things. The Lord loves His people deeply and cares for them, and therefore we felt very strongly that the Lord was saying to be prayerful and to be careful as we walk through this process of dismantling. There are many in the old structure who are needed for the new that God is doing, so 'don't damage My people by being careless'. Though we tried to take care in the dismantling process, in hindsight we could have moved even more slowly. We could have spent more time inviting our leaders and church family to wrestle with the ideas from biblical passages themselves. We could have created more space for conversations, questions and vision casting.

As well as dismantling external things, the dismantling related to our own thoughts and ideas that needed to be changed. It wasn't that everything we had been thinking was wrong, but the Lord was shifting our paradigms. He was challenging our fundamental approach and assumptions about the Kingdom and the Church. It is a helpful thing to question and challenge what we believe and why. Some of our ideas may come from our upbringing, some of our ideas may come from dysfunction, some of our ideas may come from comparing ourselves with others. The process of internal dismantling is an important one to undergo prayerfully and carefully.

Declutter

As well as the dismantling, there has been a spiritual decluttering. The Lord has dealt with ungodly attitudes in our own lives and in our spiritual family.

In Acts 27, we read about Paul on a ship in a storm. He instructs the people to throw overboard the tackle and cargo and then encourages them with these words: 'But now I urge you to keep up your courage, because not one of you will be lost; only the ship will be destroyed' (Acts 27:22). We too are being encouraged to throw overboard every unnecessary weight and excess baggage. The Lord is taking us, His Church, on a journey to become the New Testament people He called us to be. The Father loves and cares for His people and they will not be destroyed, but they must have the courage to hear and to obey. We must allow human-made structures to be broken, and we must lean on the Living Word, Jesus, in order to survive and thrive.

Practically, we have reduced our staff and adjusted our teams to make them fit for purpose in the new structure. We have sought to engage, train and mobilise more volunteers because we believe that the new things God is doing will involve far more bi-vocational people who take the mission of Christ wherever they go.

Over the years, we have started community projects, planted new campuses, remodelled old buildings and launched different sermon series. There is a real enjoyment and excitement that comes from starting new things. There is less enjoyment when it comes to bringing things to an end. It is much more difficult to recognise when something has served its time and purpose and needs to come to an end. Beginnings are exhilarating; endings can be painful. But without timely closure there can be no transition to the new thing the Lord is establishing.

Most projects, initiatives and even some relationships overrun their 'best-by date'. It takes wisdom and courage to know when something has served its purpose and to stop it before it becomes irrelevant or unhealthy. Some of what we had learned and were implementing had not come from the place of prayer and Scripture but from 'clever ideas' that we had gleaned from other ministries. There were other things that were good but had become rigid and inflexible, and these need to be refreshed and reimagined in the place of prayerful conversations. Over the last two years, the Lord has been leading us to prayerfully and carefully declutter that which is not for the next season.

One time when we were praying, Esther had a picture that we felt was a helpful way of understanding the instruction to declutter:

> I had a picture of a wardrobe. The doors were open and all of the clothes and contents were thrown out onto the floor. Everything was a mess. I knew that we needed to begin to sort through everything and only put back into the wardrobe that which fit and that which would be used. It felt like an overwhelming task.
>
> Some things that looked good in the last season were now too small and needed to be given away. Some things we would be sad to let go of, but they were no longer required for the next season. Some of the clothes were worn out and had served their purpose and so needed to be thrown out. There were still other clothes that would simply go back into the wardrobe.

This picture was helpful as we considered that the Lord seemed to be messing up our neat and tidy lives. Things that had been behind closed doors were now being brought out into the open. It was time to put things in order by the help of the Holy Spirit. Though the task felt overwhelming, it was necessary if we were to declutter and streamline what we do. The things put back into the wardrobe were only those things that were needed for the next season. Without the excess things, we would be much more free to move.

What Now?

1. Ask the Holy Spirit to reveal to you those things that need to be dismantled. Remember that this process ought to be done carefully and prayerfully.

2. Perhaps arrange meetings with your teams and those who will be impacted by any dismantling. Take time to process together what it means to dismantle old ways and rebuild new ones. Make sure the Bible is your key reference point in all decision-making.

3. Are there initiatives and activities that you or your church are doing that have served their time? Ask the Lord for boldness to bring to an end those things that are not helpful for the new season so that you can begin to declutter the wardrobe.

Prayer

If anyone builds on this foundation using gold, silver, costly stones, wood, hay or straw, their work will be shown for what it is, because the Day will bring it to light. It will be revealed with fire, and the fire will test the quality of each person's work.

- 1 Corinthians 3:12-13

Father, would You give me discernment and patience. I want to carefully and prayerfully remove those things that are no longer needed and rebuild only with that which is. Help me build on the foundation of Christ with the right materials.

Amen

Closing
Remarks

"I have found that there are three
stages in every great work of God:
1. it is impossible
2. it is difficult
3. it is done."

- J. Hudson Taylor

CHAPTER 30 - FEED YOUR FAITH

For we also have had the good news proclaimed to us, just as they did; but the message they heard was of no value to them, because they did not share the faith of those who obeyed.

- Hebrews 4:2

As we near the end of this book, it is important that you feel equipped to respond properly. It is not enough only to hear what God is saying to us; we must combine this with faith. We believe there is an important principle in feeding one's faith that leads us to inherit what God has promised (Hebrews 6:12). If we don't combine faith with what God has spoken, it will not become our reality.

We have already looked at Joshua 1 in the context of the old wineskin ending (the Lord reminded Joshua that Moses is dead). In the verses that follow this, the Lord gives Joshua incredible prophetic promises. He is told that he will be given every place where he sets his foot (Joshua 1:3) and that his territory will extend to cover a vast area of land (Joshua 1:4). As if this isn't enough, the Lord promises Joshua that no one will be able to stand against him all the days of his life and that as the Lord was with Moses, so He will be with Joshua.

Can you imagine how Joshua must have been feeling? Perhaps it is similar to how we feel when we hear the promises of God over our own life. There is a divine impartation of energy, in the moment prophetic promise is given, that kickstarts us out of apathy and into action.

We see from Joshua's response in verse 11, that he felt this impartation of faith and hope in response to the promises of God. He tells the people that they will cross over the Jordan River, in just three days, to take possession of the Promised Land. There were more than one and a half million people who needed to make this crossing. These were not all strong soldiers but families with women, children, the elderly and cattle. What is more, the Jordan River was in full flood at the time. Yet this didn't deter Joshua. He was not wasting any time. Joshua was energised by the word he had just received from God, and this led to faith in action.

As we reflect on our own journey, we can relate to the excitement and faith that Joshua had after receiving the promises. Early on, God was speaking to us so much and so clearly that we felt as though we could take on the world. There was so much hope in those early months. As the days turned to weeks, and the weeks to months, we began to hit some hurdles. There were relational challenges and financial challenges, to name only two. Suddenly, the excitement of the prophetic promises didn't seem enough to sustain our actions. We were weary, tired and questioning whether God had spoken at all. This is normal and to be prepared for.

Faith journeys, where we cannot see the full outcome but choose to walk in obedience anyway, have been normal for God's people throughout history. Hebrews 11 gives us many examples of people who lived this way. These pathways are still the way the Lord calls His people to walk today. Just as Christian, in John Bunyan's story of *Pilgrim's Progress*, had to navigate many challenges on his way to the Celestial City, it is normal, in any faith journey with the Lord, to hit rough terrain and mountainous times. 'Faith is confidence in what we hope for and assurance about what we do not see' (Hebrews 11:1).

After multiple verses of incredible prophetic promises, the Lord gives Joshua a very important command:

> Keep this Book of the Law always on your lips; meditate on it day and night, so that you may be careful to do everything written in it. Then you will be prosperous and successful.
> **- Joshua 1:8**

In other words, 'Feed your faith.' God knew that unless Joshua kept the Word of God at the forefront of his mind, he would not be prosperous and successful. It is only feeding our faith that sustains us to keep pressing on towards all that the Lord has promised. The command to Joshua stands as true for us today. We must keep God's Word in our mouths and we must keep it at the forefront of our thinking. This requires time, effort and intentionality.

The first way we can feed our faith is by spending significant amounts of time in God's Word. Romans 10:17 tells us that, 'faith comes from hearing the message, and the message is heard through the word about Christ'. When we read God's Word, our faith is fed. It is not enough to have heard the prophetic promise; we must keep on living in His written Word. We must position ourselves to hear from the Word of God every day. There have many times when our faith feels frail, and we feel weak. Opening the Bible and reading a whole book out loud individually or together causes faith, hope and spiritual strength to rise.

Another way we can feed our faith is by rehearsing the promises of God. We have found it helpful to journal prophetic words that we have been given and to read these over on a regular basis. It is also good to pray God's promises back to Him and with others. We also rehearse God's promises by sharing our story. In retelling our journey, we find that the same faith we had at the beginning starts to be rekindled in us. In fact, we take every and any excuse to tell the story of what God has said and how we are responding. This really does imprint deeply into our hearts and minds what we are doing and why we are doing it.

What Now?

1. Increase your intake of the Bible by reading an entire book of the Bible out loud in one sitting. To start with pick one of the smaller books in the New Testament.

2. Journal the prophetic promises that God has given to you.

3. Share these stories with others. Perhaps it will be around the table with your family, or maybe with work colleagues over lunch.

Prayer

Consequently, faith comes from hearing the message, and the message is heard through the word about Christ.

- Romans 10:17

Lord, thank You that faith comes by hearing Your Word. I ask for the grace to give myself to the Scriptures in a renewed way today. Forgive me where I have doubted You and help me overcome my unbelief. Help me also to learn to rehearse Your promises and prophecies and to allow them to become ingrained upon my heart and mind.

Amen

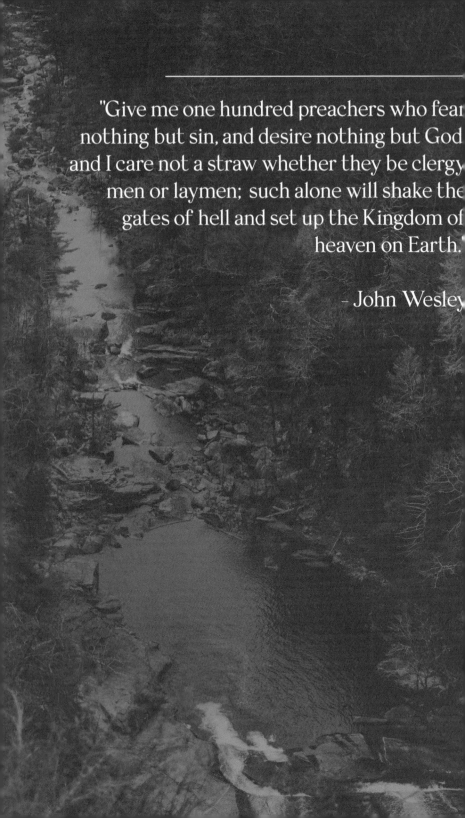

"Give me one hundred preachers who fear nothing but sin, and desire nothing but God and I care not a straw whether they be clergy men or laymen; such alone will shake the gates of hell and set up the Kingdom of heaven on Earth."

- John Wesley

CHAPTER 31 - RELEASE AND RUN

S o where are we now? We feel that we have recently entered a season of 'release'. This word comes after the sequence of words we looked at earlier in the book, 'stop, reset, recalibrate, release', and we believe that a season to 'run' is still to come.

Within the season of release, we feel that there are five distinct parts:

1. A clear vision

2. A communicable strategy

3. Right people in the right places

4. Being poised and ready

5. Divine impartation

First, we must have a *clear vision* to see where God is taking us. This is important not only for church leaders but also for those in congregations. Proverbs 29:18 (MSG) tells us, 'If people can't see what God is doing, they stumble all over themselves'. God is a revealing God, and we believe He wants us to know the destination. As an All Nations family, our vision is for all people to glorify God by knowing Christ, becoming like Christ and making Christ known. We feel we will do this as we give ourselves to making disciples and obeying the Great Commission. It is critical for everyone to both know the vision and be committed to it. This is even more important as we leave the old and embrace the new.

The second part of this release season is about having a *communicable strategy*.

> Then the LORD replied:
> 'Write down the revelation
> and make it plain on tablets
> so that a herald may run with it.
> For the revelation awaits an appointed time;
> it speaks of the end
> and will not prove false.
> Though it linger, wait for it;
> it will certainly come
> and will not delay.'
> **- Habakkuk 2:2-3**

In Habakkuk 2, the Lord encourages the revelation to be written down and made plain so that people may run with it. If the vision is where we are headed, the communicable strategy is the map to get to that destination. Having a simple and clear pathway for our church families to be a part of, so that they can know how they can engage practically, is really important.

As we have been seeking to respond to this part of release, we have been asking ourselves the following questions:

1. How do we take the person in the pew and help them to engage in disciple-making?

2. How do we ensure home churches all have the correct hallmarks and DNA?

3. Administratively, how do we manage a growing family of home churches?

4. As our American friends may say, 'Where is the on-ramp'?

A communicable strategy helps to answer these questions and allows the people to find a clear way of engaging. We have felt a warning here not to rely on human strategy that comes merely from our heads and lots of conversations. Rather, from the place of prayer and conversation between Spirit-filled people, we are to discern Holy-Spirit-inspired strategy. The Holy Spirit is often referred to as the Spirit of Wisdom. That wisdom is available to those who are listening.

We felt some parallels with the preparation that Joseph went through in the Old Testament and our own journey. After interpreting the dream for Pharaoh about a coming famine, Joseph began to implement a seven-year strategy to store up grain in Egypt. He did this even though, at the time, Egypt was in a season of plenty. It is likely that he doubted along the way whether he really had heard from God, and yet, through his obedience, vision and God-given strategy, many lives were saved.

Like Joseph, we are doing our best to prepare according to the revelation we have been given. Though it feels as though we are currently in a season of ease, and the promises of God can sometimes seem far off, we want to obey His leading and prepare new wineskin structures to handle the multiplication of souls that are coming. We must not lose sight of the vision, and we must guard against weariness in this hour.

The third part of release is about getting the *right people in the right places*. It is really important that people understand their identity, their purpose and where they fit into the bigger picture. For us, this has had an emphasis of positioning people who can bear weight in the structures that are forming. We are living in one of the biggest shifts of people in the body of Christ as people are being moved and joined as the Spirit leads. For some, this has meant a geographic relocation and for others an internal repositioning. We must all remain flexible and continue to listen to the Spirit. God is spiritually joining people, even those who were formerly strangers, and realigning people so that everyone is playing the role they ought to be playing.

This movement can expose insecurities and so is an opportunity to deal with internal health and issues that may not have been evident before. Joel 3:11 talks about warriors quickly assembling from the nations and the Lord bringing down His warriors. This is a time when people will know their places and will be called into the right places by the Lord, with no jostling.

The fourth part of the season of release is about *being poised and ready*. Like a runner on a racetrack who hears the words, 'On your marks, get set…', we feel we are being invited to live ready by keeping our ears attentive and waiting for the 'Go'. The runner on the blocks is not doing multiple other things but has a keen awareness of the race ahead and has a single focus. Practically, this speaks into the importance of fixing our eyes on Jesus and remaining in an intimate place with the Lord. Much more is said about this in Chapter 16, 'Fix Your Eyes on Jesus', and Chapter 9, 'Invitation to Intimacy'.

The fifth and final part of the season of release is about *divine impartation*. As we embrace extended periods of time in prayer, fasting and reading the Word, we will know a strengthening that will help us to be ready to run. We have sensed a particular promise from the Lord that He will strengthen our legs ready to run, that He will strengthen our voice so that it will carry a fresh power to change lives, neighbourhoods and regions, and that He will sharpen our eyes to see prophetically and awaken our ears to discern the times. All of this divine impartation comes from extended periods of time with the Lord. Whether individually or as a community, we must create space and time to encounter God. Ephesians 6:10 says that we are to be 'strong in the Lord and in his mighty power'. It must become normal for Christ-followers to spend extended periods of time in prayer and in Bible intake. This has been the way of Christians throughout history but is not so common for people today. However, this is changing and a new breed is emerging.

The season to run will follow the season of release and is a time for giving ourselves fully to all the Lord has revealed and helped us put in place. As shared in Chapter 18, the Lord spoke to us in May 2020 and said, 'It will take two years to turn the ship [All Nations] around and then you must give the next three years to really become established into the new you have embraced.'

As a spiritual community, we have just begun to enter this phase of our new wineskin journey. Our mindset is like a marathon runner who has been trained, focuses on the destination, has a clear understanding of the path to take and settles in for the run ahead. This will be a time of Holy Spirit activity where disciples are made and churches planted. We are believing for signs, wonders and miracles to become a common occurrence again. The Lord always saves the best wine till last. We can be confident that what He will do in the days to come will surpass what He has done before. They will be glorious times, and yet some of the most challenging too.

What Now?

1. Pray through the five parts of the season of release and ask the Holy Spirit for understanding and wisdom on how this translates in your context.

2. Take this chapter and read and discuss its context with your spiritual community as you discern its implications for the wider Church.

Prayer

Therefore, since we are surrounded by such a great cloud of witnesses, let us throw off everything that hinders and the sin that so easily entangles. And let us run with perseverance the race marked out for us,

- Hebrews 12:1

Father, thank You that You are an advancing, moving God. Please help me to understand the ways of Your Kingdom and to align my life so that I may run into all that You have for me.

Amen

"It is about the greatness of God,
not the significance of man.
God made man small and the universe big
to say something about himself."

- John Piper

CHAPTER 32 - YOUR STORY IN HIS STORY

S o what does this mean for you who are reading? Perhaps you have read this book and are tempted to see it as simply a new idea or model of doing Church. Perhaps you feel as though the revelation within it has been specific to our context and journey alone. We pray that you will see that stories live within stories; they are woven, like a beautiful tapestry, into one another. They cross barriers of culture, class and geography and span centuries in time.

The Kingdom coming, making disciples and planting churches continues a story that began in the Garden of Eden. It was in the Garden that humans first had relationship with the Father, and ever since the Fall, God has been wooing people back to Himself. We see from Jesus' prayer in John 17 that it is still the heart of the Father to be one with His people. God is raising up communities across the globe to do just that. Whether it is with All Nations or another organisation or family, we are all invited into the glorious mission of God.

We don't believe it is an accident that you have read this book, and we pray that you will see the invitation of the Father to get caught up in the big story that He is writing. It is only in the context of God's bigger story that our individual stories make sense, take on meaning and find their significance.

~

We felt it was a prophetic sign that our eldest daughter Bethany helped us to finish this book just days before giving birth. Our prayer would be that, as you reach the end of this book, the early signs of labour would begin, you would embrace the discomfort and your life would be forever altered as we usher in the new.

FURTHER READING

RESOURCES ON DISCIPLE-MAKING

Online Resources

All Nations Movement Resources for an apostolic tribe committed to making disciples and planting churches. Available at: https://allnationsmovement.org, as well as ANstorehouse.org

All Nations Movement Disciple eCourse. Available at: https://ANstorehouse.org/course/disciple

Disciple making resources, articles and books. Available at: https://discipleship.org

Disciple Making Movement software. Available at: https://Disciple.tools

Discover App - The Discovery Bible Study App for Android and iPhone. Available at: https://discoverapp.org

e3 PARTNERS Training Resources for Disciple Making Movement. Available at: https://e3partners.org/training-resources

Generation Mapper – Assessment tool for coaching church planters. Available at: https://genmapper.com

Zúme Training online resource for disciple training in small groups. Available at: https://zume.training

Books

Addison, Steve (2012). *What Jesus Started: Joining the Movement, Changing the World*. Downers Grove, IL: IVP Books.

Allen, Roland (2006). *The Spontaneous Expansion of the Church: And the Causes That Hinder it*. Cambridge England: Lutterworth Press.

Galanos, Chris (2018). *From Megachurch to Multiplication: A Church's Journey Toward Movement*. Lubbock, TX: Experience Life.

Moran, Roy (2015). *Spent Matches: Igniting the Signal Fire for the Spiritually Dissatisfied*. Nashville, TN: Thomas Nelson.

Smith, Steve with Ying Kai (2011). *T4T: A Discipleship Re-revolution*. Monument, CO: WIGtake Resources.

Watson, David and Paul Watson (2014). *Contagious Disciple-making: Leading Others on a Journey of Discovery*. Nashville, TN: Thomas Nelson.

RESOURCES ON REVIVAL

Online Resources

'Billion Soul Harvest: Interview with Mike Bickle' [Video] YouTube, 21 May 2022. Available at:
www.youtube.com/watch?v=VxazUrMRjqo

'Behold the Bridegroom Cometh-Julie Meyer' [Video] YouTube, nd. Available at: www.youtube.com/watch?v=6DuXD6DSTms

All Nations Movement Revival Ready eCourse. Available at: https://anstorehouse.org/course/revivalready

All Nations Movement Revival Podcast. Available at: https://anstorehouse.org/videoresources

Books

Bounds, E M (2019). *Power Through Prayer*. S.L.: Bibliotech Press.

Liardon, R (2003). *God's Generals: The Roaring Reformers*. New Kensington, PA: Whitaker House.

Liardon, R (2008). *God's Generals: The Revivalists*. New Kensington, PA: Whitaker House.

Pratney, Winkie (2002). *Revival: Principles to Change the World*. Pensacola, FL: Christian Life Books.

Smith, Oswald J (2003). *The Revival We Need*. Buckingham: Rickfords Hill Publishing Ltd.

Trousdale, Jerry (2012). *Miraculous Movements: How Hundreds of Thousands of Muslims Are Falling in Love with Jesus*. Nashville, TN: Thomas Nelson.

RESOURCES ON THE APOSTOLIC

Online Resource

The Peace Apostolic website has many rich articles and teachings See
www.peace.org.au/apostolic.html

Book

Alley, John Kingsley (2002). *The Apostolic Revelation: The Reformation of the Church*. Rockhampton, Qld.: Peace Publishing.

RESOURCES ON HUMILITY

Mahaney, C J (2008). *Humility: True Greatness.* Colorado Springs, CO: Multnomah Books.

Murray, Andrew (2018). *Humility: The Beauty of Holiness.* CreateSpace Independent Publishing Platform.

APPENDIX A
PROPHETIC REVELATION GIVEN TO
JEAN DARNALL, 1967

During those weeks a vision came to me. It appeared three different times, during prayer, and it was the same vision each time. Now most of my revelation from the Lord is what I just 'know': He makes me know something, and I speak it forth. But now and then I have a vision, and when I do, I have a pretty good one! Some people have a very garden-variety type of visions: they're getting them all the time, you know. But I just have them now and then. And it's usually a milestone: a turning point or very large directive in my life.

And what I saw was the British Isles, as in a bird's eye view. A kind of haze was over the whole, like a green fog. And then little pinpricks of light began to appear from the top of Scotland to Land's End. Then the Lord seemed to draw me closer to these lights, and I saw that they were fires that were burning. They were multiplying from the top of Scotland to Land's End. Then I saw lightening come and strike those fires, the brightest spots particularly, and there was a kind of explosion, and rivers of fire flowed down. Again, the sense of direction was from the top of Scotland to Land's End. But some of those rivers of fire didn't stop there. They went right across the Channel and didn't stop there. They went right across the Channel and spread out into the Continent.

The third time this vision appeared I figured the Lord was showing me or trying to tell me something. I was in Dorset by this time, at St Mary's (Church of England) with Rev Ken Prior, and I asked him if I could stay an extra day. You know, there's nothing quite so awkward as an evangelist the day after the meetings are over. But I said, 'Could I stay an extra day in the vicarage and pray? I need to find out what the Lord is trying to say to me.' Because up to that point I was really still on my way to Hong Kong. And the Lord spoke to me very clearly. It was a wonderful day. It certainly changed the path of my life.

When I say the Lord spoke to me, I don't mean that it was an audible voice. But it was a knowing. That strong knowing, like reading at the end of a book and knowing exactly what was going to happen. And you can't change it: it is written. And so it was written upon my heart, the meaning of this vision.

Phase One: The Glowing Fires

The Lord impressed it on my Heart that those fires I saw were groups of people whom He would make intensely hungry for New Testament Christianity. They would start reading their Bibles and saying, for instance, as they read the book of Acts, 'Well, where is this happy church? Where are these people so full of the power of the Holy Spirit? Where are these miracles? Where is this growth, this vitality, this courage, this boldness that these people had? Is that for today – can we have it today? Should the Church be this way?'

And as these questions were being planted in their hearts, the Lord Jesus said He would make them very hungry for the Holy Spirit; He would fill them with the Holy Spirit, and out of those gifts would flow ministries that would enrich the Body of Christ. The whole concept of the Body of Christ would come alive, and barriers between denominations and different types of Christians would break down as people met each other. The Lord said He would move these people all over the country. After He had taught them gifts, He would move them to another place where they would carry that fire, and where they would meet others also who were being renewed by the Holy Spirit. He would put them in different situations from what they were used to, so that they would get to know people of other denominations, other cultures and other classes, and be able to communicate to them the blessings that the Lord had given them. And then He told me that during that time He would also test them. There would be great testing of faith, great waiting times. He would teach them spiritual warfare. He would show them the meaning of the power of the blood of Jesus, the name of Jesus, the Word of God and the power of the Holy Spirit.

Phase Two: The Coming of the Lightning

Then I asked the Lord, 'What does the lightning stand for?' And He said, 'Unlike the first part, in which I will be speaking to Christians and preparing My Church and renewing it and reviving the saints, the lightning represents a second part of the vision, in which I will bring a spiritual awakening to the nation that will be a witness to the unsaved, to the un-churched, to the non-Christian.'

'Through these believers I will bring a witness to this land. They will be an army of witnesses. And I will begin to release their ministries so that when they give their testimonies there will be apostolic signs following and accompanying their testimonies. Where ears have been deaf and hearts have been hard and eyes have been blind, I will touch the people of this land and they will begin to hear the testimony of My people, they will begin to see the manifestations of My power, and their hearts will begin to believe. Thousands and thousands of people are going to come into my kingdom through this army of witnesses, through this people movement – not characterised by any particular evangelist or great organisation at the front, but just My people rising up, led by My spirit and beginning to move forward with a new faith for evangelism, a new zeal to share Jesus with others. And as they give their testimonies, I will release their ministries of healing and miracles, and there will be signs and wonders accompanying their ministries. So many people will be saved, in the villages as well as in the cities, in the schools, in the government, in media, in industry. It will affect the destiny of this nation; it will determine the course of the times.'

Phase Three: Streams across the Channel

Then I said, 'Lord, what about these streams that go on across the Channel into Europe?' And He said, 'That represents people who will rise up in the midst of this people movement, this army of witnesses in Britain, whom I will make My communicators.' Now I hadn't used that word very much before in ministry I said, 'Lord, what do you mean by communicators?' And He said, 'They will not only be people endowed with the gifts of the Holy Spirit, with strong faith, but they will also be people talented in the arts. They will be writers, musicians, singers and actors, and also technicians in television, radio and the mass media. I will call and send them and put them in strategic places. I will bless their natural talents with My Spirit, and they will be good: they will excel. They will be leaders in their fields. I will send them into Europe, where they will meet other people in the media, and through them I will release the word of God very fast in Europe. The result will be another wave of a spiritual awakening, with thousands coming to Christ throughout Europe.' Well, I got kind of excited after I'd heard all that from the Lord, and I said, 'Lord, why are you telling me this? I'm on my way to Hong Kong.' And He said, 'Oh, no you're not: you're going to stay right here, and I'm going to bring Elmer here.' And I said, 'What do you want us to do, Lord?' And He said, 'I want you to nourish the fires that I light.' So I'm not the firelighter. The Lord is the Firelighter.

A Time of Waiting

My husband was in Hong Kong another year before he got here. But when he came, several pastors asked him if he would start a school for leadership training for people who had been filled with the Spirit and had gift ministries. He said, 'Well, I'll set it up for a year, and then we'll go back to the United States.' We forgot that we didn't have anything to go back to – you know, we'd sold the house and given away everything. I had given the money to the poorest people I could find – young preachers just starting out in the ministry. So there was nothing to go back to. But we still had that mind-set. It took a little while for the Lord to make us realise that He had other plans.

That was twenty-one years ago. And during those twenty-one years I have ministered all over this country, as Pastor Black has mentioned. But I have never gone away up to the north of Scotland. Many times I've said to my husband, 'I'd just love to go up there and find the fires that God has been lighting.' And he has said, 'Well, why don't you g o on? I don't mind, if you want to get ahead of the vision.' You know, it's very easy, when you get a revelation from God, to think you've got to go out and make it happen. That's very unwise – it doesn't bother God much but it sure can be embarrassing for you. You can fall flat on your face. I've tried that a couple of times, and I think I've learned my lesson on it. So I said, 'No, I don't want to do anything like that. I want to go when the Lord really calls me to go, if He needs me.'

A Brush with Death

Last August, our college sponsored a conference with a wonderful man of God named Judson Cornwall. Just before he came, I collapsed in a church service with a near-fatal coronary. Graham Kendrick was standing beside me; I was so glad he was there because he prayed for me right away and I was wonderfully touched: instantly the pain subsided. It took me a little while, though, before I got home. I thought I had a bad case of indigestion! But the Lord did heal me, and I was able to attend the conference.

And a Revelation from Heaven

And one day, between lunch and the afternoon session, I said to our team, 'Let's just pray before we go upstairs.'

I was thinking about very matter-of-fact things like how long should the worship go on, and where would we take the offering and so on. I certainly wasn't thinking about the visions and lights and fires. And suddenly the Spirit of God came upon me. I don't know if you've ever had anything like that where God's power and presence comes on you so mightily that suddenly everything else is forgotten. It wasn't that I couldn't have stopped; but I didn't want to. I began to weep and weep, and strong crying came upon my heart, real, deep sobs. I knew that the Spirit of God had brought the Lord's burden upon me. And I said, 'Lord, what is happening to me?' The closest thing I could compare to the intensity of the anointing that was upon me at that moment was when the Lord called me into the ministry when I was only fifteen years old. And I said, 'Lord, what is this? It's something very important.' One word He spoke to me: 'Scotland'.

Phase Two at Hand

Scotland. I knew what it meant. I knew that He wanted me to come up here, and I knew that He wanted me to come up with a special message. That message is to say to as many people as I can, in as many places as I can, that the second part of that vision is right at hand. It's here, folks, that spiritual awakening: it's starting; the very first signs of it are already upon us. Your generation are going to see a harvest of souls in this land such as you have never seen before. And it's going to have a tremendous effect not only upon this nation and the British Isles, but upon many other nations.

The First Sign: Men at Prayer

There are three things that the Lord has asked me to share about this vision everywhere I go: three signs of this awakening. The first is that the Lord is sending a strong call to prayer among men. Early Morning Prayer meetings will start all over the land as men desire to pray, and they will start asking their pastors and leaders, 'Can we meet together before work and pray?' In those prayer meetings, there will come strong intercession and an increased faith and vision in these men's souls for the nation. They will not only pray in their own churches, but soon they will start combining together in other churches, with other church groups. And in some places these prayer meetings will grow too big for the building, and they will come out in the open and pray in the parks or in front of town halls.

Wouldn't that be nice, to have a prayer meeting right out here, of hundreds and hundreds of men lifting their voices in prayer for the nation? And it will be a sign in itself: these prayer meetings will be a witness to the nation, and many people will come to the Lord just by witnessing these prayer meetings, and hearing the prayers of these men.

The Second Sign: Christ Revealed to the Young.

The second thing is that the Lord is going to send a tremendous revelation of Himself to boys and girls in this country. Between the ages of nine and fifteen particularly, children will begin to have a revelation of Jesus. They will see Him, they will know Him, they will hear Him, He will speak to them. He will come to them in visions and dreams, He will reveal His word to them. They will be converted and filled with the Holy Spirit and gifted by Him. And they will start praying. They will be healed themselves, and they will start praying for each other; and there will be wonderful healings through these boys and girls.

They will not only be the children of Christian parents. The Lord is going to manifest Himself to those who are in non-Christian homes where there is no love nor real family unity, where there is no knowledge of the Lord at all: perhaps not only for one generation but for many generations, no Christian person has been in that family. But Jesus is going to meet them and reveal His power and His presence to them and His love for them. When they start coming to our children and to our teachers and telling what they are seeing and hearing from the Lord, our duty will be to receive them and love them as they are- because they will be rough diamonds, and they will have rather unusual, un-churchy language. But their experiences will be real. Some of their experiences will be so unusual you may doubt them. At that point receive their testimonies at face value, give them the Word of God, and teach them how to love: because these children will have ministries not only as children, but as leaders in their adult life, and they will bless your country and other countries. So receive these children, teach them. Those of you who teach Sunday school, those of you who have children in your home and neighbourhood whom you are concerned about, begin to ask the Lord to raise your level of expectation of what they can receive, because they are going to start hearing. And just like the adults, they will start hearing the word and receiving the Lord and being able to receive deep spiritual experiences in the Lord.

The Third Sign: Anointed Preachers

The third thing the Lord said He would do relates to the raising up of preachers. Although this awakening will not be characterised by great evangelists at the beginning, it will produce great preachers. You are going to hear evangelists with such fire, such powers of persuasion that they will touch thousands of people and win them to the Lord Jesus. God is giving these preachers not only to Scotland; He will send them to other parts of Britain, and many to other parts of the world, with an ever-increasing ministry of winning many people to the Lord.

Beware of Jealousy and Criticism

When the Lord reveals something to you, then you pray into it, not to make it happen, but to pray that as many people as possible will be involved and touched, and hear. And when I pray for this particular part of the vision, for these preachers and evangelists, I just feel the sorrow of Jesus' heart, for He says to me that He has already given to this land in recent times good ministries, strong ministries, that He wished to increase, but they were cut off, and hindered, and narrowed in the dimensions of their greatness because of jealousy, criticism and envy. In my spiritual warfare I have been coming against that spirit of jealousy, envy and criticism – because I think that it will try to rise up again, even in the face of the tremendous anointing God will give these preachers. So I just ask you to be on guard, be alert to that, and if you feel those feelings and emotions rising up in you against some ministry that God is blessing, be generous in your heart, be quick to repent of it, and ask the Lord to take that away, so that you can contribute and nourish and support those ministries, rather than stand back from them with hostility and jealousy. The Lord is going to use them whether you like them or not. But it would be a lot better if you liked them and got right there beside them, because then you could share the joy of winning souls for the Lord Jesus – because that's what it's all about, folks.

The Lord isn't sending us for fun and games, any more then He sent the charismatic renewal for us to have holy huddles and exchange spiritual gifts like Christmas presents all the time. That isn't the purpose of the renewal. The purpose is evangelism. It's to get out there into that harvest that God is preparing. And you sons and daughters of Scotland will be part of a modern ministry movement that will bless the whole world, and Scotland will greatly contribute to this. So be part of it.

A Deluge of Power

You young people, you are going to see miracles and effective ministry such as our eyes have never seen, as the Lord pours out His Spirit, not only upon the Christians, but upon the unsaved, in these days. So be encouraged. Jesus said men ought always to pray and never give up – because this harvest is bound to include some of your friends, some of your neighbours, your families, who need the Lord. So have faith, have courage.

Take Courage

When I first came to England, Jeanne Harper met me, and drove us from Heathrow in a little Mini car, riding on the wrong side of the road, you know! My daughter and I had five pieces of luggage each – we thought we needed all of that – and so the car was heaped up inside and out with all this luggage. As Jeanne was driving furiously through the peak hour traffic, my heart was thumping, first because I was excited to be here, and secondly because of all the traffic and double-decker buses and everything.

I looked out over the tops of the cases and saw a great big red sign with gold letters saying, 'Courage! Take courage!' And I said to her, 'Isn't it wonderful how your government has put up all these morale boosters!' She said, 'Oh, these are ale advertisements.' I said, 'Oh, well, I'll take it in the right spirit!'

So have courage, folks: take courage, and know that God is with us, and He has chosen to cause our eyes to see things that He has prepared for us in this age that are beyond anything we could ask or think. He will do it, according to the power that works mightily in us as His Church. Praise the Lord.[24]

---

[24] Hugh Black, *Revival: Including the Prophetic Vision of Jean Darnall* © 1993. Used by permission of New Dawn Books, Renfrewshire, PA15 1XX.

APPENDIX B

Prophetic Revelation Given to Pastor David Minor, 6 April 1987

Blessing and Judgement with Increased Anointing

The Spirit of God would say to you that the wind of the Holy Spirit is blowing through the land. The Church, however, is incapable of fully recognising this wind.

Just as your nation has given names to its hurricanes, so I have put My name on this wind. This wind shall be named 'Holiness unto the Lord'.

Because of a lack of understanding, some of My people will try to find a shelter from the wind, but in so doing they shall miss My work. For this wind has been sent to blow through every church that names My name. It shall blow through every institution that has been raised in My name.

In those institutions that have substituted their name for Mine, they shall fall by the impact of My wind. Those institutions shall fall like a cardboard shack in a gale. Ministries that have not walked in uprightness before Me shall be broken and fall. For this reason man will be tempted to brand this as a work of Satan, but do not be misled. This is My wind!

I cannot tolerate My Church in its present form, nor will I tolerate it. Ministries and organisations will shake and fall in the face of this wind and even though some will seek to hide from this wind, they shall not escape. It shall blow against your lives and all around you, some will appear to be crumbling, and so they shall, but never forget that this is My wind, saith the Lord. With tornado force, it will come and appear to leave devastation, but the Word of the Lord comes and says, 'Turn your face to the wind and let it blow,' for only that which is not of Me shall be devastated. You must see this as necessary.

Be not dismayed, for after this My wind shall blow again. Have you not read how My breath blew on the valley of dry bones? So it shall breathe on you. This wind will come in equal force as the first wind. This wind will also have a name, it shall be called, 'The Kingdom of God'. It shall bring My power. The supernatural shall come in that wind. The world will laugh at you because of the devastation of the first wind. But they will laugh no more, for this wind will come with force and power and will produce the miraculous among My people and the fear of God shall fall on the nation.

My people will be willing in the day of My power, saith the Lord. In My first wind that is upon you now, I will blow out pride, lust, greed, competition and jealousy, and you will feel devastated, but haven't you read, 'Blessed are the poor in spirit for theirs is the Kingdom of Heaven?' So out of your poverty of spirit, I will establish My Kingdom.

Have you not read, 'The Kingdom of God is in the Holy Ghost?' So by My Spirit, My Kingdom will be established and made manifest. Know this also. There will be those who shall seek to hide from this wind and they will try to flow with the second wind, but they will again be blown away by it. Only those who have turned their faces into the present wind shall be allowed to be propelled by the second wind.

You have longed for revival and a return to the miraculous and the supernatural. You and your generation shall see it, but it shall only come by My processes, saith the Lord. The Church of this nation cannot contain My power in its present form. But as it turns to the wind of the Holiness of God, it shall be purged and changed to contain My glory.

This is judgement that has begun in the house of God, but it is not the end. When the second wind has come and brought in My harvest, then shall the end come.

Further resources by Steve & Esther Uppal can be found at
www.steveuppal.com

Find out more about their ministry, All Nations Movement - an apostolic tribe commited to disciple making and church planting. Visit **www.allnationsmovement.org** for more information.

There are further resources on revival, disciple making and church planting available for free on the All Nations learning platform, Storehouse.
Visit **www.anstorehouse.org**